Praise for AMERICAN DIPLOMAT

"Since 1916, State Department special agents have protected our nation's secrets and diplomats around-the-globe. AMERICAN DIPLOMAT is a window into the dynamic and complex world of protecting diplomats, defending embassies, combating terror, hunting spies, and investigating complex international crime. Read Alex's story, you won't be disappointed." — *Fred Burton, former special agent and New York Times best-selling author of Beirut Rules, Chasing Shadows, Ghost, and Under Fire.*

"AMERICAN DIPLOMAT, though a biographical novel, unveils the story of Alex Reinshagen's service to our country - from a law enforcement officer to landing a position as an honored and decorated Security Officer in the United States Diplomat Corps. Though fictionalized for security reasons, his journey rings true throughout his story. You will discover a world few get to see or experience about the trials and tribulations involved in protecting our country's diplomats. Well done!" — *T.M. "Mike" Brown, Southern Author of The Last Laird of Sapelo, Sanctuary, Testament, and Purgatory. President Emeritus, Hometown Novel Writers Association, Inc., and Newnan Carnegie Library Foundation Board of Trustees.*

"In my forty-year newspaper career, I have met several government agents. After reading AMERICAN DIPLOMAT, I'm convinced I finally know one now. Alex Reinshagen has given us a rare look at what goes on behind the scenes that most of us only catch fleeting glimpses of on the news. His story will not disappoint." — *Vince Vawter, author of The Paperboy Trilogy (Paperboy won a prestigious Newbery Honor in 2014).*

"We can follow the movements of history both through the press and through books. However, we seldom have access to the daily activities of those who participate in the frontline of vital events. Alex Reinshagen offers us that insight. As a special agent of the Diplomatic Security Service of the Department of State, Reinshagen describes his professional and life trajectory from his beginnings as a police officer in the heart of the country to the most important outposts of American diplomacy. Written in an engaging and straightforward style, with the truthfulness of a protagonist endowed with exceptional powers of observation, this book allows us to glimpse, from Israel to China, the plots that today define the battle against the enemies of the West." — *Miguel Cossio, Chief Operating Officer of AMERICA CV NETWORK. Senior Media Executive with over thirty years of industry experience as a director, producer, journalist, and writer. Awards/Accolades include Emmy, Telly, AP, and international Awards.*

"With AMERICAN DIPLOMAT, Alex Reinshagen gives an impressive as well as informative *behind the scenes* look into the fascinating world of foreign service and international diplomacy - it is an intriguing read from start to finish." — *Johnathon Scott Barrett, author of the award-winning novel, Ship Watch.*

"In a book full of adventurous and sometimes hilarious tales of a life in the foreign service most of us can't even imagine for ourselves, Alex Reinshagen recounts the personal dream he followed and the physically and psychologically intense journey that ensued for him. The vignettes he relates will inform, surprise, and transport readers. A fascinating work!" — *Carol Johnson, bookseller, Commonplace Books, Oklahoma City*

"AMERICAN DIPLOMAT is an amazing story. It is very relatable and an informative read. The book shows us how important resilience and adaptability are when undertaking a career of public service. Alex is a brave man for taking on the task of writing his memoir!" — *Mark Slater, MBA, Canberra, Australia*

AMERICAN DIPLOMAT

Alex B. Reinshagen

Moonshine Cove Publishing, LLC

Bowling Green, Virginia U.S.A.

First Moonshine Cove Edition June 2024

ISBN: 9781952439834

Library of Congress LCCN: 2024911530

© Copyright 2024 by Alex B. Reinshagen

Cover and interior design by Daniela Reinshagen, Ph.D.

I dedicate this book to my wife, Daniela, who is my editor, cover designer, and publicist as well as my best friend and dream girl. She encouraged me to write my story and worked countless hours making it better and more enjoyable for my audience while helping me write an exciting and interesting memoir. This is her book as much as it is mine.

About the Author

Alex Reinshagen is an international security leader with a 26-year career in firefighting, criminal law enforcement, immigration law enforcement, and global security operations. Before becoming a police officer in South Carolina and US Border Patrol Agent in California, studies at Northern Kentucky University and the University of South Carolina propelled him to join the US Department of State as an American Diplomat. After serving in Thailand, Egypt, Slovakia, Bangladesh, Palestine, Iraq, Israel, and China, he retired as the senior State Department liaison at FBI Headquarters and is now the Managing Director of Viking Security Consulting LLC and a contributing writer for The Bruges Group in London. He lives on St. Simons Island, GA with his wife and their youngest son, where he is writing his next book.

AlexReinshagen.com

Preface

After twenty-six years in firefighting and law enforcement, having lived abroad for twelve years and visited over seventy countries, I decided to retire from the US Foreign Service and leave the lifestyle that came with it behind. I had reached the turning point and wanted to change the direction of my life and slow down. To do that, I needed to clear my head, free myself of all the *mental weight* that kept me awake at night. Putting it all down on paper, capturing my stories, thoughts, and concerns, seemed like the way to go. I wanted to write my story. But not for everyone, for me. Just so I could sleep at night. I wanted to put it in writing so I could rest and not think about what I had done, accomplished, not accomplished, screwed up, or when I had done the right thing. *Maybe one day, my wife and kids could read about my career and, to some degree my life, and see it from a different perspective.* But I didn't initially plan on others reading it. Then I thought, *why not?*

I have as many interesting stories to tell as you care to hear, and perhaps, others should know the commitment it takes to be a part of the Diplomatic Security Service and the United States Foreign Service. My wife, Daniela, encouraged me to write my story and get it published, and the result is on the pages to follow. Her editing of my manuscript improved the book to the point that I could approach a publisher with a finished product. If it wasn't for her abandoning her career in Slovakia and leaving her friends and family to explore the world with me, I wouldn't be the man I became. I owe everything to her.

This is a book of memories and tales. Some of it is fiction and some is fact, but all of it is based on real-life experiences. Much of what I did throughout my career was classified at the Secret or Top-Secret level, especially while living and working in Iraq and China. I can't get into details. Naturally, some names, dates, and locations of my accounts have been changed due to the sensitivity of the circumstances. Or have they?

AMERICAN DIPLOMAT

1
The West Bank

It was my first trip to Ramallah. Westerners traveling into Palestine from Israel — or from anywhere for that matter — was a rare occasion. Retired US General Anthony Zinni was scheduled to return to the West Bank town to meet again with Yasser Arafat, the President of the Palestinian National Authority and Chairman of the Palestine Liberation Organization. The aim of the meeting was to broker a cease-fire between the Israelis and Palestinians and finalize the release of five Palestinian militants who had been convicted of killing Israel's Tourism Minister, Rehaveen Ze'evi, at the Hyatt Hotel in Jerusalem in October 2001. I was on the US team assigned to transport the prisoners from Arafat's housing compound known as the Muqata'a to an Israeli jail in Jericho, a shanty desert town two hours to the southeast. I figured this assignment was going to be exhilarating, but I didn't know we'd be making history. It was May 1, 2002.

A month earlier, I arrived in Tel Aviv on a temporary-duty assignment from the US Department of State's Diplomatic Security Service Washington Field Office. It was a routine assignment, and it was my turn to go. It was April, so the Mediterranean would be pleasant. In less than eighteen months after beginning my career as a Special Agent with the Diplomatic Security Service, I had seen and done more than I ever thought I would do while growing up on the west side of Cincinnati. This assignment in Israel added to my already thrilling career as a Special Agent in the US Foreign Service.

Leaving the Washington Field Office, I took my Sig Sauer P228 9-milimeter government-issued pistol apart, putting the slide and magazines in one of my bags, the barrel and frame in another, and packed it into my checked baggage, just the way we were taught at the academy. The United Airlines flight to Tel Aviv from Dulles

International Airport outside of DC was long, but as I was eager to get to the Middle East, the time went by quickly. Upon arrival at Ben Gurion International, I proceeded through the Diplomatic Arrivals Lane at the immigration checkpoint and showed my black US Diplomatic Passport, which could get me into almost any country in the world quite easily, with royalty treatment to boot. Carrying a diplomatic passport was a huge honor and privilege that only a few select people get the chance to do.

At baggage claim, two Israeli immigration police officers approached me and asked if those were my bags, pointing to my cheap American Traveler luggage on the carousel. "Yes," I replied. After presenting my black passport and collecting my luggage, the officers searched my bags and located the gun parts I secreted in various interior pockets. Much to my surprise, and contrary to what I had been advised to do previously, the officers coolly informed me that I didn't need to dismantle my pistol before packing it into checked baggage. Rather, I could have kept it together, but I should have placed my gun in a lockable container inside my checked bag.

"Fair enough, am I free to go?"

"Of course," was the reply. "Welcome to Israel."

Walking outside the terminal, I found my embassy-appointed driver and off I went to the US Embassy in Tel Aviv to check-in with the Regional Security Officer who was also a Special Agent with the US Department of State's Diplomatic Security Service. The American Embassy in Tel Aviv was a heavily fortified compound a block away from the warm, blue water of the Mediterranean Sea. Since I had been with DSS for less than two years and didn't have much experience working overseas, the RSO ignored me for the most part during my temporary-duty assignment. I didn't take it personally, though. I was just another agent, making my way around the world, filling gaps that needed filling. Well-trained, armed, and ready to eat glass if the boss told me to, but just another warm body, nevertheless. A mouth-breather working *blood-money* assignments so I could save some cash and buy a nice BMW or townhouse in one of the many Northern

Virginia suburbs just outside of DC. Hell, I loved it. It was my dream job and I got lucky I was selected to join the Department.

During my first week or so in Israel, I mainly assisted in running protective security operations down to Gaza. These security details were always fun and were a young man's job. They required an agent to be extremely fit, dedicated, well trained, and work long days on little sleep.

"Grab an Uzi and as many rounds as you can carry, Alex. We're taking the AID Chief to Gaza today and the CIA is coming with us," one of the more senior DSS Agents assigned to the embassy as an Assistant RSO would tell me. In this case, *senior* meant the agent had been in the Department for three or maybe four years compared to my paltry eighteen months. But since it was my first time in Israel, and only my second foreign trip as an agent, I respected someone who had the balls to ship off and live in a different country. That's why we joined, and before long, I would be moving overseas, too, but I didn't know where or when that might be. For now, I was happy escorting the chief of the US Agency for International Development to the northern edge of Gaza. Why he was going, I didn't know and didn't care.

"Any Uzi?"

"Yeah, any that have a number taped to the barrel. If a name is on it, they've been assigned to someone posted here. The rest are spares, so grab one with a number."

"Roger that, and what's the load-out?" I asked, wondering what type and how much ammunition I should take with me.

"As many magazines of nine-millimeter ball ammo you can carry," the senior agent replied. "Oh, the spares have never been zeroed so good luck hitting anything with that piece of shit unless it's standing right in front of you."

Outstanding.

I went to the armory and selected an Israeli-made Uzi sub-machine gun and six or seven magazines of 9-millimeter full metal jacket ammunition for the Uzi and 9-millimeter hydra-shock bullets for my Sig Sauer P228 pistol — the type of bullet with a hollow point that cause a great deal of tissue damage upon impact with flesh and are designed to stay inside the body and not pass right through it. This would ensure as much damage to body tissues and internal organs as possible.

Working security details in the US meant wearing a suit and tie, but in the Middle East, the typical agent attire consisted of beige cargo pants and short-sleeved plaid shirt, untucked and long enough to cover the pistol and magazines, pepper spray, handcuffs, and flashlight. Hiking boots were part of the unofficial uniform, too, and maybe a baseball cap. Oh, and Oakley sunglasses. DSS Agents — the guys anyway — always wore Oakleys. That was our calling card. We could always identify the DSS Agents because they were wearing Oakleys. The Secret Service Agents didn't wear shades. It was just one of those things.

The Director of the US Agency for International Development, or USAID, was Andrew Natsios during the Bush Administration. The plan was to head to the northern border of Gaza from Tel Aviv, forty-seven miles to the south. My job on that day was *left rear*, a knuckle-dragger position in a protective detail motorcade of armored vehicles. In this case, they were black Chevy Tahoes, fully armored to lessen the impact small weapons fire could have on the occupants. This meant the windows were bullet-proof and inside the door panels steel plates were affixed to the frame and the pillars to keep bullets from entering the inside of the vehicle.

Dressed in the typical DSS casual attire, I collected my gear from the armory without signing for a damn thing and headed toward the three-vehicle motorcade in the parking garage of the embassy. The embassy has since been designated by former President Donald Trump to be in Jerusalem, or J-Town as it was known, but for now, it was in Tel Aviv. By this time in my career, consisting of nine months of training and nine months on the job, I had worked dozens of protective security details in DC and New York, protecting foreign diplomats traveling to the United States and the US Secretary of State, Madelaine Albright. It was nothing new, but it was my first time in Israel, so I was a bit nervous about heading to Gaza.

I was the last guy to meet up with everyone else at the motorcade. "Reinshagen, you're delaying our departure. Hurry up. Fuck."

The Gaza Strip in 2002 was recognized as a Palestinian-occupied territory controlled militarily by Israel. Overcrowded and hot as hell during the summer months, Americans entering Gaza were an obvious target. I guess that's why we never entered. We parked in a lot just north of the border while the AID Director's counterpart came across the border and met with the director in a dilapidated building on the Israeli side. That was fine by me.

"Sit tight," said the Tactical Commander of the protective detail, or simply *The Detail*. The DSS Agents, me included, were eager to roll into Gaza to protect the Director, but since we weren't going to cross the border into Gaza due to a logistical change made on the fly, we stayed by our motorcade and waited for the meeting to adjourn and eventually made the drive north to the American Embassy. What we thought would be an exciting and memorable day in the Gaza Strip turned into yet another *hurry up and wait* day in Israel.

After a couple of weeks of menial embassy security operations such as running *intruder drills* with the US Marines who were there to help the team of DSS Agents protect the embassy and classified information inside, we got word retired US General Anthony Zinni was scheduled to return to Jerusalem the following week. We were going to take him into the West Bank town of Ramallah to meet with Yasser Arafat and assist in the peaceful turnover of a handful of Palestinians who were tried and convicted in absentia of the murder of the Israeli Tourism Minister.

During a Monday morning staff meeting, the RSO talked about the upcoming operation.

"Reinshagen, you're going to Ramallah tomorrow, to Yasser Arafat's compound. It's under siege by the Israeli Defense Force and is under constant watch by a dozen news outlets. *Al Jazeera, CNN, BBC* — a lot of cameras, so stay sharp. You're going to be taking one of the Palestinian prisoners from the Muqata'a, which is where Yasser Arafat is being kept quiet by the IDF, in a motorcade to a jail in Jericho run by the Israelis. You're qualified on the M-4, right?" the RSO asked, ensuring that I was legally permitted to carry a Colt M-4 carbine rifle, and handled it well enough to be trusted to fire it.

"Yes, sir."

"Good. Leave the Uzi behind. Nine-millimeter rounds aren't going to do any of us much good in the desert. Pack a bag and go down to motor pool to get a ride to Jerusalem today. You have reservations at The David in J-town. I'm not sure when you're coming back to Tel Aviv. Get with Miller and Carpathia after this meeting for logistics."

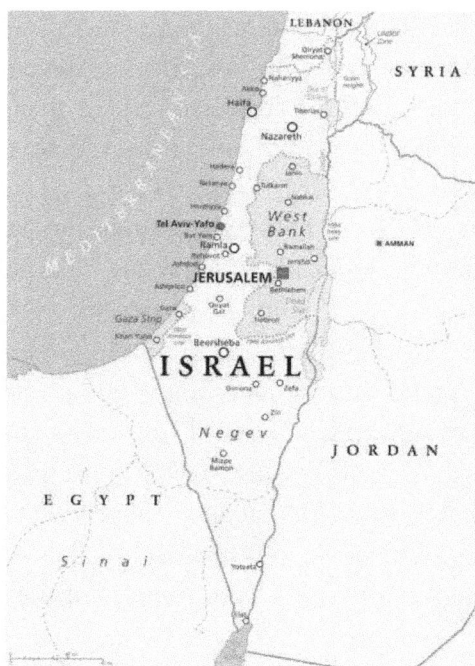

The King David hotel in Jerusalem was the crown jewel of hotels in the city. Not a bad place to be if you ever find yourself visiting this historic city and its *Wailing Wall* separating West Jerusalem from East Jerusalem.

Miller, Carpathia, and I were the temporary DSS Agents in Israel on a sixty-day assignment, helping the American security team ensure a vehicle bomb didn't pull up outside the Embassy in Tel Aviv or the

Consulate in Jerusalem and explode. If prevented, then our assignment was successful, and we could go back to whatever field office in the US we came from, only to be replaced in two months by another rotation of agents from the US. Roger Miller and Ben Carpathia graduated from the academy six months before I did. I'd never met them until this trip, but working long hours during assignments, we get to know the agents we work with pretty well.

Ben Carpathia was my height — six feet tall — but weighed two hundred twenty pounds. He wasn't muscular, but he also wasn't overweight. He was somewhere in between. Born and raised outside of Atlanta, he graduated from the University of Georgia, and got hired by GBI, Georgia Bureau of Investigation, the state police agency. He had a Georgian drawl when he spoke, making him sound like a country boy and had a dry sense of humor. Later in his career, he was assigned to the US Consulate in St. Petersburg, Russia, married a pretty Russian woman who was obviously out of his league, and they had two children together. He once showed me a picture of his wife and I teased him that there is no possible way a cute Russian woman would marry a neanderthal from Athens, Georgia, like him. Hell, people probably thought the same thing about me when I married the prettiest woman in Central Europe. We both got lucky. Luck is underrated.

Miller grew up in North Miami Beach, Florida, and graduated from Florida Atlantic University with a Sociology degree. He became an Immigration Inspector in Miami for the US Immigration & Naturalization Service before joining DSS as a Special Agent and spoke fluent Spanish, which was a bit unusual because of his green eyes and alabaster skin. He was a family man who went to church on Sundays and was a damn good investigator. We got along immediately.

The M-4 carbine rifle is a gas-operated, American-made assault rifle which shoots 5.56-millimeter bullets and is accurate as hell; much better for long-distance engagement with nefarious actors who may want to get a jump on our motorcade. But the likelihood of the Palestinian militants, both ill-equipped and poorly trained, from stopping our armored Suburbans and Tahoes was unlikely. This *movement* from

Jerusalem to Ramallah to Jericho and back was going to take five or six hours. Five DSS Agents were going, plus five embassy-trained Israeli Defense Force drivers, former Shin Bet agents who were operating the armored SUVs, and everyone was carrying as much firepower as possible.

Ramallah is a god-forsaken section of the desert about twenty kilometers north of East Jerusalem, in a territory known as the West Bank of the Jordan River. The West Bank is the largest of the landlocked territories claimed by Palestine and borders Jordan to the east and the Dead Sea to the south. Ramallah is home to thousands of Israeli citizens in addition to 2.5 million Palestinians.

The Muqata'a compound in Ramallah was built in the 1930s by the British as a military headquarters, a court of law, and a prison. In 1948, the Kingdom of Jordan took over occupation and used the facility as a prison and a home for Jordanian army officers. After the *Six Day War* ended in 1967, it became an Israeli military headquarters until the Palestinian Authority was created in 1994. It wasn't until 1996 when Arafat moved in and made the Muqata'a the official military headquarters of the West Bank and established control by the Palestinians.

Retired US General Anthony Zinni had met with Arafat in January 2002 and again in March. The goal of this upcoming meeting was to negotiate a peaceful transfer of five Palestinian men who were tried and convicted in an Israeli court of the murder of Israeli Minister of Tourism, Rehavam Ze'evi at the Hyatt Hotel in Jerusalem in October the previous year. The five gunmen fled to Palestine. Ze'evi was a well-liked official who grew up in Jerusalem and became a platoon commander in the IDF and, eventually, Chief of Staff. The Popular Front for the Liberation of Palestine claimed credit for his murder and stated it was in revenge for the assassination of Abu Ali Mustafa who was killed earlier that year. Ze'evi was honored with a military burial in Mount Herzl in Jerusalem. Thousands attended. After the killing, the Israelis placed Arafat under siege in Ramallah to force the transfer of the five gunmen to Israel. On March 29, 2002, the IDF raided the Muqata'a compound and placed it under siege during *Operation Defensive Shield.* Israeli soldiers destroyed half the buildings on the compound including a guesthouse, sleeping quarters for Palestinian guards, a kitchen, and a large meeting hall.

During the meeting that took place in April 2002, the General Zinni-led entourage brokered a plan in which the suspects would be held in an Israeli jail in Jericho and guarded by American and British forces. General Zinni was slated to return to Ramallah a month later, under a full protective detail led by the State Department's Diplomatic Security Service, or DSS. The high-threat operation was not the first time DSS was involved in an operation of this magnitude, and it wouldn't be the last, but it would certainly be historic.

After the RSO meeting, I met with Miller and Carpathia to discuss weapons needed for the trip to Ramallah, our required load-out, and transportation from Tel Aviv to Jerusalem. All of us went back to our hotel just down the street, packed some clothes and energy bars, and returned to the embassy later that afternoon to catch a ride fifty miles east to Jerusalem. A beautiful and ancient city located on a bluff overlooking the adjacent city of East Jerusalem, the history there was astounding. But we weren't there to be tourists. This trip was different. After checking into our rooms at The David, the finest of the hotels in the city, we were picked up by a consulate driver in an armored Tahoe and taken to the consulate to meet with the RSO.

Mac was a big man. He was six feet four, had square shoulders, and looked like he played college football before becoming a Special Agent fifteen years prior. Like the RSO in Tel Aviv, Mac ignored me at first but warmed up to me as the days passed. Later in life, we even became friends. After retiring from DSS years later, he returned to local law enforcement and wore a uniform for the Arlington, Virginia, police department.

We were briefed by Mac and his assistant, another Special Agent named Cates, about tomorrow's operation to Ramallah. Ted Cates joined DSS a couple of years before me and was on his second tour of duty. His first was on the Secretary of State's Protective Detail when Madeleine Albright was America's top diplomat. Standing nearly six feet and cleanly shaven with a handsome smile, the female agents were always keen to talk to him. He was from Pittsburg, graduated from Penn State in the Reserve Officer's Training Corp, then became an officer in the Marines. After four years in the Marine Corp, he joined the FBI and later transferred to DSS. He was skilled with weapons and was the best marksman I'd ever met. Unfortunately, some years later, DSS put him on the *rubber gun squad,* meaning he was suspended from his job, with pay, because he was arrested for domestic violence. DSS Agents, like every other law enforcement officer in the country, are not authorized to carry a gun if they are convicted of this crime, so any allegation of DV, whether it was true or not, was career-ending because it tarnished an agent's reputation and followed him wherever he went. Although his wife later recanted the story that he had beaten her, and dropped the charges against him, the damage had been done. DSS was skeptical and considered him a bad seed. Right or wrong, that's the way DSS works. Cates was forced out and later got hired by the Naval Criminal Investigative Service as a Special Agent. The last I heard; he was assigned to the American Embassy in Rome.

Cates provided a bit of history in the region, showed us a presentation of where we were going, the number of vehicles in the motorcade, what problems could arise, where the nearest hospitals were located, the rules of engagement with any enemy we might come across, logistical considerations, and the timeline. *A walk in the park, right?* We were scheduled to leave the next morning at 9:30 a.m. in a six-vehicle motorcade of armored, Level-D Chevy Tahoes. *Level-D* armored vehicles are like tanks; heavy as hell, difficult to stop once you got them moving, and armored on all sides of the car — both sides, front and back, roof, and undercarriage.

"You guys are qualified on the M-4, correct?" queried Cates.

We nodded our heads in agreement.

"Good. I'll check out the long guns to you tomorrow. We're using blue tip 5.56-millimeter rounds, and we have a hundred or so magazines already loaded. Carry what you can. We're rolling into Ramallah under IDF protection since they control the area. Arafat's compound has been under siege for weeks, so you'll see a lot of Israeli tanks and a lot of media, but they aren't allowed too close to the Muqata'a. We're going to maneuver our motorcade into this courtyard," Cates explained as we concentrated on his presentation.

"These two buildings are the only buildings occupied by Arafat and his guys. The rest of the buildings are occupied by the Israelis. The courtyard is the drop zone, adjacent to the front door, located here," Cates continued, showing us the location where the Shin Bet drivers would park, and we'd exit the vehicles.

"Once we make it to the courtyard, Mac will send each of us into the Muqata'a, one-by-one, to take control of a prisoner or two. You'll bring your guy out through this door and down the steps to the motorcade, which needs to be restaged for a clean exit heading back the same direction you entered. Are we all clear on this? There's only one way into this courtyard and the same way out."

The three of us nodded, "Clear."

"We're taking five convicted killers out of the building, loading them up into separate Tahoes, and getting on the road to Jericho as quickly as possible. Reinshagen, you're bringing out the last guy. He is the worst of the bunch. If the Palestinians are going to go after any of the vehicles, yours is the one they'll likely go after."

"How many guys does Arafat have in this building?" Carpathia asked.

"We don't know for sure, but we think thirty to thirty-five, according to satellite imagery and IDF reports."

"Weapons?"

"AK-47s, some small arms, we can't be too sure. The IDF wants this to go smoothly so they don't have to light this place up with 120-millimeter tank rounds after you guys pull out. Be sure you wear your plates and helmets and take extra batteries."

Wearing *plates* meant inserting heavy iron shields into our body armor carrier to help protect our vital organs from heavy weapons fire. In theory, these plates would stop an AK-47 bullet, but no one wanted to test that theory. Especially not under these circumstances. The extra Motorola radio batteries would be necessary if our walkie-talkies, or WTs, ran out of power. Communication devices and weapons were the most important things to have during operations like these. Without either, we could find ourselves in serious trouble.

The next morning, everyone assembled at the US Consulate. It was 8:00 a.m., the sun was shining, and the temperature was quickly rising. It was going to be a scorcher in the desert. We met Agent Cates in the armory and were issued our M-4 rifles and plenty of ammunition. After another briefing by Mac and the Consul General, who is the top-ranking US Diplomat in the Consulate, we filled our Camelback filtration devices with cold water and loaded our Tahoes with weapons, an automated electronic defibrillator, night vision equipment and meals ready-to-eat, then got ready to roll. Six cars, all armored Chevy Tahoes. Only five vehicles were actually needed to successfully complete the mission, but one was assigned as the lead car, or the vehicle in the lead position of the motorcade which was to be used to ram any unexpected roadblocks we might come across or could be used in the event one of the other five Tahoes would break down, get a flat tire, or be shot to shit by the Palestinians.

"It's going to get hot today," said one of the local Israeli criminal investigators assigned to the security team at the consulate.

"Miller is from Miami, so he's used to the heat. Right, Miller?" teased Cates. "Time to roll. Let's load up."

Each of us got into the front right seat of our Tahoe and conducted radio checks, ensuring our WTs were powered and on the correct channel. The Motorolas were set to *talk-around* which meant the radio frequencies we were using were short-wave. The communications would be limited from one WT to another, as opposed to using the long-range frequency which travels from a user to a repeater or antenna located on the top of the embassy or a hotel in the city, then back down to the rest of the WTs within listening range. Since we were going to be in the desert, radio-to-radio communications would work best.

At 9:30 a.m., we started to move through town in the direction of East Jerusalem and toward an Israeli checkpoint leading into a section of the West Bank controlled by the Israelis. The Muqata'a, however, was in a smaller district under the control of the Palestinians. I use the term *control* loosely here, as the Israeli Defense Force could have taken over the Palestinian territory including the Muqata'a anytime they wanted, but since Israel has a lot of enemies throughout the Middle East, playing nice was the thing to do. For now.

"Don't show your weapons at the checkpoint, gents," Cates squawked over the radio to all ten vehicles in the motorcade; six were ours, and the other four were occupied by Israeli paramilitary mercenaries and the Brits, who drove the first car in the motorcade; a Range Rover. Only five, however, were occupied by Americans — five DSS Agents, General Zinni and his right-hand man, the Chief Political Officer from the US Department of State posted at the US Consulate in J-Town, and the Consulate's Chief Medical Officer.

We slowly approached the first Israeli checkpoint departing East Jerusalem. Heavily armed Israeli soldiers checked us over, identifying everyone in the diplomatic-plated vehicles. Thanks to our Shin Bet drivers, the Israeli equivalent to the FBI, we sailed through rather quickly. All ten vehicles stayed close together as we descended a dirt road leading us into the desert, surrounded by a sea of beige sand as far as we could see.

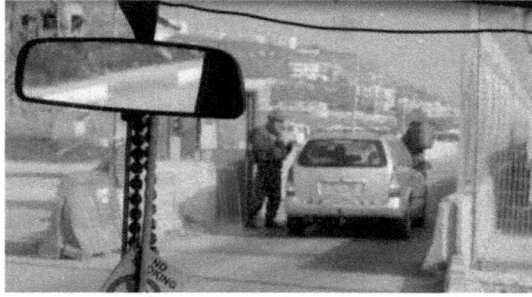

Thirty minutes or so later, we approached the Palestinian stronghold of Ramallah, a small city in the middle of nowhere loaded with news station vehicles from around the world — American, British, Australian, French, Brazilian, Japanese, Chinese, Russian, even a Canadian news crew was there to film the American motorcade enter the Muqata'a compound and take custody of the five men wanted by Israel. As we approached our destination, forty-plus Israeli Merkava tanks lined the streets in and around the Muqata'a. Twenty thousand Israeli troops had been deployed throughout the region once the siege against Arafat began earlier that year. A couple of tanks blocking the street backed off as our motorcade rolled past on the dusty road, only to re-position once again, ensuring our safety. The image was surreal.

As we pulled our vehicles closer to the courtyard, several Israeli military Humvees pulled aside, allowing the six armored US Tahoes to pass unabatedly, circling in the courtyard, and coming to a stop in front of the main entrance leading to Arafat's haven, just as Cates had shown us on the presentation.

Heavily armed, I exited my Tahoe, as did Carpathia and Miller. Cates and Mac emerged from their vehicles as well. Since the Israelis took control over most of the compound, their soldiers occupied the building across the courtyard. I looked up, checking to see how many friendlies had my back. Most of the windows were open, with armed Israeli soldiers waving and taking pictures of us and our Tahoes, happy we were there to take control of the prisoners and hand them over.

"All right, here's the play," said Mac, standing on the front steps of the Muqata'a, his bald head glistening from the sweat. "Cates goes in first and brings out the first two prisoners. Next up is Miller, then Carpathia, then Reinshagen, retrieving one each. Once Alex gets his guy in his vehicle, he'll let me know, and we roll out. All ten cars will remain in the motorcade all the way to Jericho. Any questions?"

Hell, I had a few questions but wasn't about to ask. *Where are we going once we got in the front door? Do we have radio comms inside the building? Should we search our guy for weapons, or are we blindly taking custody of a Palestinian prisoner from the Palestinian military inside the Palestinian Army Headquarters based on trust? What are the rules of engagement?* I think Miller felt the same way. I could see the brief confusion on his face as he gave me a pointed look, before composing himself again. But no, I wasn't about to ask then. I should have asked at the briefing the day prior. *Whatever, let's just get on with it. And don't fuck it up.*

While Cates entered the Muqata'a to get the first two prisoners, Miller, Carpathia, and I waited by our Tahoes, itching to see inside the building where Arafat has been in hiding. About twenty minutes later, we heard some chatter on the radio coming from Mac, who was tensely waiting for Cates to reappear from the maze of hallways inside the Muqata'a and walk down the stairs to the foyer and main entrance.

"Coming out with two," Cates whispered into his Motorola radio.

"Roger that, clear out," Mac replied from the front steps, ensuring it was safe for Cates to exit through the front entrance and make his way to the motorcade.

Cates stepped through the main entrance of the Muqata'a, escorting the first two of the hand-cuffed Palestinian prisoners, and accompanied by a couple of guys dressed in clothing consistent with the local tribe. He walked his guys down the stairs just outside the main entrance and put them into the back seat of the second Tahoe in line. The first Tahoe was the lead car. Mine was the sixth car, the one in the back. After Cates got into the front right seat of his Tahoe, Miller stepped into the foyer and was met by an Israeli interpreter from the US Embassy in Tel Aviv. They chatted for a few seconds, but I couldn't hear what they were talking about. From the looks of it, the *terp* was providing Miller with directions on how to get to where he needed to be to link up with his prisoner, who was somewhere inside the huge, beige concrete block building.

Ten minutes later, Miller spoke into his Motorola, "Coming out with one."

"Roger, clear out," I confirmed from the front steps, keeping my eyes peeled and head on a swivel.

Same as Cates, Miller escorted his prisoner down the steps and into the back of his Tahoe.

Carpathia was next. But this time, it took about forty-five minutes before he came out with his guy.

"Did you have tea with the guy, Carp?" Cates joked over the radio.

"Tea and crumpets. The Brits left some behind when they pulled out in '67."

"Slight change of plans, gents," Mac was heard saying on the Motorola from somewhere inside. As we looked back toward the front door in unison, we realized Mac was nowhere to be seen and must have entered the building, but why we didn't know.

The location of the prisoner I was to bring out had changed. An interpreter described over the Motorola where in the building I should go to get my guy. I followed the instructions, or so I thought. I entered the building and walked upstairs, like I had been instructed. Several hallways and half a dozen turns later, I found myself in a skywalk, an enclosed skybridge separating the Muqata'a from the building across the courtyard occupied by Israelis and stopped dead in my tracks. As I stood in the doorway staring into the faces of a room full of soldiers from the Palestine Liberation Organization, all carrying weapons, I realized I must be in the wrong place. I was scared shitless. The stench inside the room was almost unbearable and I wondered when the last time was these soldiers took a shower. The room was warm, which didn't help, and I felt the sweat rolling down my back. What seemed like minutes was probably only a few seconds before I recovered from my initial shock and started gathering my thoughts. My eyes trained ahead of me, I got on the radio and tried to reach Mac to let him know I was lost, but there was no response. *Damn!* The signal was not going through. I retraced my steps in my head, realizing I was given the wrong directions by the interpreter.

Weighing my options, I figured my best course of action was to get the hell out of that room and back to where I came from. Tightening my grip on my rifle, trying to steady my breathing, I slowly backed up and made my way down the hall, hoping no one would open fire. I could hear my heart skip a beat. With the American flag on my body armor and Kevlar helmet, it was obvious who I was and why I was there, and I guess that's what kept me alive.

I got on the radio again, trying to reach the interpreter, and to my relief, this time he responded and directed me to the right location. After circling back through a couple of corridors on the third floor, I made it to the conference room where he was waiting for me, and I recognized the room from television newscasts. It was the conference room where Yasser Arafat was always filmed. A few seconds after I arrived, a couple of Palestinian soldiers with rifles walked over to me and said in Arabic something to the effect of, "Don't get near him." I wasn't sure who they were talking about until I saw Yasser Arafat walking down the hall toward me. He walked right by me and turned right, into the conference room where General Zinni was already seated.

After ten or so minutes of further negotiations, my terp turned to me and said, "He's all yours." *He*, meaning the final prisoner we needed to transport. "We already searched him," the IDF one-star general said to me as he nodded at Mac, and we walked toward the stairs.

Typically, DSS Agents only trust other DSS Agents about life-safety issues such as searching a prisoner for weapons. If another agent tells me he searched a guy, I'd use my discretion on whether I search the guy myself. If I trusted the agent to search someone correctly, then maybe I wouldn't do it again. In this situation, I made a judgement call to get the hell out of the Muqata'a as fast as possible with my prisoner. I figured once I made it to the motorcade in the courtyard, I'd search the prisoner myself.

With an expression of defeat on his face for having to turn over his men to the enemy, Arafat looked at me and then my prisoner before being escorted down the hall by his militia. I grabbed my prisoner by the shirt collar with my left hand, keeping my right hand on my Sig, still holstered, and nodded at the terp as if to say, *Let's get out of here.* We exited the conference room and walked down a few flights of stairs to the building's foyer. I was anxious to get on the road and put some distance between us and this place.

"Two coming out, plus one," I radioed to the other agents as we crossed the main entrance floor.

"Clear out."

Once Mac and I made it to my Tahoe, I did, indeed, search the prisoner to ensure he didn't have any weapons or explosives. I wasn't going to take chances with this guy. If the Palestinians wanted to cause the Americans harm during the transport, this was the guy they'd use to get the job done. Once I was satisfied he was clean, I nodded at Mac, and he gave me the thumbs-up to load my prisoner into the armored Chevy Tahoe. I placed him in the right rear seat and fastened a seat belt around him. I got into the left rear seat, staying unbuckled, and got ready to leave while Mac got in his Tahoe and said *slow roll* over the Motorola.

The first Tahoe began slowly pulling forward, followed by the others in a single-file line the way protective security details typically depart a site. As all the vehicles exited the courtyard, I looked up at the IDF in the open windows of the building situated next to the Muqata'a. I remember seeing some of the Israeli soldiers taking pictures of us and waving as we left, and I realized just then how historic this moment was. I tensed up for just a second then relaxed a bit as I shook my head in disbelief as to what we had just done and where we were headed. We picked up speed, met up with the other four armored IDF and protocol vehicles, turned left on to the main dusty road in town, and headed south toward Jericho.

Once we got to the outpost in the desert located near the Dead Sea, we began unloading our prisoners. American and British security forces at the jail, who had been assigned to guard the prisoners, approached the motorcade, looking over the five Palestinians, waiting for their chance to conduct a thorough search of each. Just then, as I got my guy out of my Tahoe, someone fired a pistol. For a second, I thought we were under attack by Palestinian militants determined to take back what was theirs. Everyone ducked, taking cover behind an armored car. But then I realized one of the Israeli guards assigned to the Jericho jail fired his pistol into the ground by accident, nearly shooting himself in the foot. "ND!" I yelled, letting the Americans know one of the guards just discharged his weapon due to his lack of training or carelessness. "Careful with the weapons, gents!"

We handed over the convicted felons, got back into our Chevys, and made our way back to the Consulate in Jerusalem before heading west to the Embassy in Tel Aviv. We unloaded our equipment and weapons, had a de-brief with the RSO about the operation, and walked down the street to our favorite Vietnamese restaurant for dinner. I got back to my hotel room just after 11:00 p.m.

The next day, as I was getting a coffee at the embassy cafeteria, one of the Israeli locally employed staff told me I was on the front page of the *Tel Aviv Times* that morning.

"Really? I didn't know."

"Yes, go buy a copy. Your face was blurred out, but it was you."

"How do you know it was me?"

"Because you were the only blonde in the entire West Bank yesterday."

"Why'd they blur my face?"

"For your safety. If the *Times* didn't blur you out, you'd have to get out of Israel. You're a wanted man in Ramallah, my friend. Don't go back there."

Outstanding.

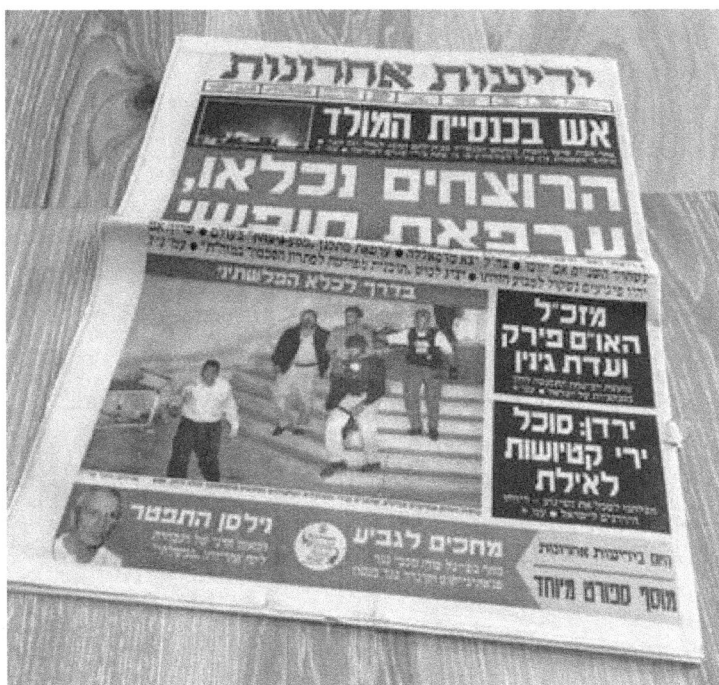

A couple of weeks later, I saw on the news that the skywalk I entered — the room that was filled with Palestinian soldiers — no longer existed. The IDF bombed the shit out of the place, and it came tumbling to the ground. I must've been the last Westerner ever to step foot in that room.

The phrase *slow roll* can be used in a few situations, but I'm neither a poker player nor a pilot. When I talked about a slow roll during this protective detail operation in Ramallah, I was referring to a phrase used by agents indicating it is safe and time for the lead vehicle to slowly pull away from where the motorcade is parked, and the rest of the cars to follow, until all the vehicles are moving forward, going in the right direction, and no one is left behind. The agents in the motorcade keep their eyes open, watching out for suspicious people, vehicles, and fast-approaching traffic which might be an attack or common road rage. Once the vehicles are all moving together, with the correct amount of distance between each as to ensure other cars never enter the motorcade at any point, the lead car begins speeding up. At that point, the rest of the vehicles in the motorcade pick up speed, staying in a compact formation, one behind the other.

DSS Agents are some of the best federal agents when it comes to driving at fast speeds, because we got a lot of training and practice working in teams while protecting, or guarding, the US Secretary of State and foreign diplomats who have come to the United States to meet at the White House, State Department headquarters, the Pentagon, or any number of government buildings, restaurants, and hotels. It's common for DSS protective motorcades to pick up a Foreign Minister at Dulles International airport, get on Interstate 66 eastbound, and drive eighty miles per hour with only a few feet separating our bumpers in a three-vehicle motorcade as we make our way to the Ritz Carlton in Georgetown or to the White House for a meeting with the US President.

Slow roll also has another meaning to me, more personal. A career in the United States Foreign Service, which is a division of the US Department of State, whether a Special Agent, Economics Officer, Facility Manager, or Ambassador, requires us to move around the world, taking one assignment after another. We know this going into it. And after a few moves, a lot of people decide it isn't for them, so they transition to another government agency or the private sector. Hell, I thought about getting out of the State Department several times because of the constant moving every two or three years. But it was also a lot of fun. The job never got old because I was always moving to a new city or country. For every country I moved to, it would take months to figure out how to get an internet connection, where the best grocery store is located, who to trust at work, and how to get things done. Every new assignment began with a slow roll before I could pick up the pace and get things done and live comfortably in whichever country I happened to be living at the time. Take it easy at first, spot the potential obstacles, make sure I'm heading in the right direction, then pick up speed, work hard, make an impact. Then get reassigned to another city or another country, just to do it all over again.

2
Doogie Howser

Let me take you back to the beginning.

Born and raised on the west side of Cincinnati, being the youngest of ten kids had its advantages, but also disadvantages. There was always someone around the house and I learned from my older siblings, simply by observing, the right and wrong ways to do things. I had a great childhood. As with every other child growing up in the Midwest, I didn't learn a thing about religion, money, or sex. And like every other child, I had to figure it out on my own. Attending a public school, it was common for catholic families to send their kids to the local catholic private school every Wednesday morning before the public school opened to attend a catholic sermon in a classroom and, sometimes, in the church itself, presided over by a nun or priest. Every few months, we were forced to confess our sins to a priest in a robe, in the private confessional at the back of the church. I must have been ten years old at the time, confessing sins that only a ten-year old had to confess.

"Forgive me, Father, for I have sinned. My last confession was three months ago," I'd whisper to the priest sitting in the booth next to me, separated by a screen.

"Go on."

"Um, I … I called my brother a jerk because he...he wouldn't change the channel to MTV," I stuttered, scared out of my mind that I'd be doomed to eternal hell for this horrible act.

"Ok, son. God has forgiven you of this sin and you are cleansed of all unrighteousness. Sit in the front pew and say five Hail Mary's for your absolution."

Yes, we were the family that went to church every Sunday to pray to an unknown God for continued shelter and food, and the love of our family. When I was fourteen, my older brother was given the unenvious

31

responsibility of taking me to mass on a Sunday afternoon. I had a baseball tournament earlier that morning and missed the morning mass. Instead of taking me to church, we went to K-Mart and shopped.

"Aren't we going to church?"

"This is church today, little man. Relax and look around. We'll go home in forty-five minutes."

I didn't think going to K-Mart was a good idea, but I kept my mouth shut and did what he told me to do. When we returned home, my mother asked how church was, and I couldn't bring myself to lie to her. I told her my brother took me to K-Mart, and we skipped mass. I wasn't sure if he would get in trouble over it, but figured our mother would not let it go, and I felt like such a shit for throwing him under the bus. One could argue that his actions put me in a bad position of choosing between lying to my mother, and not breaking my brother's trust, but I didn't see it that way. Like I said, I was a good kid, and I had my eyes on the prize — follow the rules and become a police officer. But I also wasn't going to stab a friend in the back again, like I did to him that day.

Years later, when I was a grown man and had lived overseas for several years, my father told me a story about a conversation he had with a priest in that same church. You see, my siblings and I attended public school. The catholic schools in our neighborhood, including the boys' school, Elder High, and the girls' school, Seton High, were quite expensive for my parents to send all of us. My oldest brother was the only one of us who attended the private catholic school. The rest of us had the pleasure of a public education. It's not as if we were poor — far from it! But my mother raised ten kids while my father worked his behind off, only to come home each night and have a hotdog or peanut butter and jelly sandwich for dinner so the rest of us could eat hamburgers or spaghetti. He sacrificed a great deal for us. They both did.

"John," one of the priests said to my father one day at church, "I don't see any of your boys going to Elder. Why aren't you sending them to catholic school?"

"Well, Father," my dad replied, "I can't afford it. I have a lot of kids."

"I see. I think you're going to have to make some sacrifices so you can afford to send them to Elder High."

I can only imagine my dad, thinking to himself, *You must be out of your mind to think I haven't sacrificed enough to raise ten good kids.* After that conversation with the priest, I think my parents started backing away from the Catholic faith and the church.

Like most houses in the Midwest, ours had a basement. It was *finished*, meaning it had carpeting and a television, a couple of big sofas, and the laundry room. Our basement had dark wood paneling on all the walls and god-awful carpeting with square colors of orange, brown, and white. I loved it back then. I'd play with my Matchbox cars on the carpet and remember I had a police car and a police motorcycle that I was obsessed with. At the age of five, I already knew what I wanted to be for the rest of my life — a police officer.

I figured myself lucky to know at such a young age. Most people have no idea what they want to do in life until they go off to college. Even then, many are just figuring out what they like, what they are good at, what their passion is, what they want to learn more about, and spend their lives doing. Not me. I knew early on, and I focused on it my entire life. I wanted to join the Cincinnati Police Department. So, I walked a chalk line growing up, never getting into any trouble, doing the best I could in school. I was a B student, and that was alright with me. Once I got to high school, I'd see marijuana being passed around at parties in the neighborhood from time to time. I sort of wanted to experience it, but I didn't want to blow my chances of realizing my dream of becoming a cop by getting arrested for possession of drugs, so I politely waved off the offers to smoke a joint when it came my way. It was good that I did.

When I was a high school senior, my parents bought a small horse farm across the border in Indiana. As much as I didn't want to move with them to Indiana, I had to. I continued going to my school in Ohio, though. I'd drive across the border to attend school, then drive back to

Indiana at night to study and work. Yes, I was a good kid for the most part and had my eyes set on attending college, which my parents never encouraged me to do and couldn't pay the tuition. Thus, I worked my ass off at the local lumber yard while attending Northern Kentucky University, a forty-five-minute drive from home. The winters in the Midwest can be bone-chilling and my old Datsun didn't have a good heater, so I'd drive to my college classes with a blanket over my legs just to stay relatively warm. It was a piece of junk, had well over three hundred thousand miles, but it was all I could afford to buy on my own. It even left me stranded on the highway once after breaking down. I had to get it towed to the nearest Sears to get it fixed, and that cost me money I certainly didn't have. I remember asking my father for a five-thousand-dollar loan so I could buy a used pick-up truck. I made my case — I was getting all A's in my college classes and working thirty hours every week at the lumber yard, but he wouldn't lend me anything. I wasn't sure whether my parents had the money to loan me, but assumed they did. I really don't know why, to this day, they wouldn't. But after that, my dad didn't talk to me much. He mainly stayed out of my business and never asked me how school was or what my plans were after college. I once asked him if I should take ROTC courses and go into the military after college.

"Army or Air Force?" I asked him.

"Air Force."

He never brought it up again. I always thought that was strange. He never offered advice and we never discussed my future after that. Not once.

I told this story to a friend recently. I pondered out loud why my dad didn't encourage me a bit more to go into the Air Force. He never sat me down and told me the pros and cons of military life and which department I should join. I figured he'd have an opinion since he joined the Army after high school, trained in Texas and served our country in Massachusetts from 1955 to 1957. I asked, but he didn't seem to care at all. My friend told me maybe my father didn't want me to join the military and that's why he didn't encourage me or discuss it at all. That had never crossed my mind, ever. It was a revelation to hear a different side of the story — maybe this is exactly what my father was thinking. I spent my entire life wondering about that. I figured he was too tired to deal with me after raising my nine siblings. I can't blame him. But he didn't want to talk about it, didn't want to think about it, and didn't care what I did. I thought he just wanted to be left alone, in his new basement with new carpeting, and new television, so he could watch Tom Brokaw on *60 Minutes* in peace and quiet, and not deal with a college kid. To this day, I still don't know what my father thought about the path I took as an adult. He died three years ago.

My dreams had changed quite a bit since I turned five years old playing in my basement, and I started thinking about joining a federal law enforcement agency. After taking criminal justice courses for four years, I wanted to continue my education at graduate school, but couldn't afford it, certainly not after having paid for my undergraduate degree. Nevertheless, I took the entrance exam for graduate school and applied to Florida State, Notre Dame, South Carolina, and North Carolina, hoping that I'd earn a scholarship. Without that, I couldn't pay for further schooling and would have to simply join Cincinnati PD, my original dream job. But I was not giving up yet and, as it turned out, there was more in store for me after all. A few weeks later, I was accepted into the graduate program of Criminology at two of these schools. I was invited by the University of South Carolina to come down for an interview to be a Graduate Assistant, which meant I would work in the security field while attending college on a scholarship. The interview went great, and I left campus feeling pretty good about myself. I drove north to the University of North Carolina campus to have a look around, my hopes up, trying to decide whether I should attend South Carolina or North Carolina. But first, I needed a scholarship offer. Without financial assistance, I'd stay in the Midwest, become a police officer where I grew up, and life would be just fine, I told myself.

Two weeks after I returned to my parents' house in Indiana, I got a call from the University of South Carolina. They offered me a full scholarship as a Graduate Assistant. I accepted the offer on the spot.

They wanted me there as soon as possible. *I did it!* I was so happy. A week later, UNC called and offered me a full scholarship to their Criminology program, too. *How great was that!* Over excited, I turned the offer down, having already committed to USC. I was going to be a Gamecock and, eventually, a police officer, or maybe even a federal agent, just as I had always known, since I was five.

I always thought that I was so fortunate to have known what I wanted to be at such an early age. Some kids wanted to be firefighters or lawyers, or they wanted to play center field for the Cincinnati Reds. I wanted to get into law enforcement and made sure that everything I did in life led me to becoming an officer in uniform. How many are fortunate to know this at five? But...was I really that fortunate?

To decide there and then, in my basement with the dark paneling on the walls, the smell of mold after a heavy rain, playing with my Matchbox police cruiser? I think back about it now and think maybe it was foolish. Maybe I should have been open to other opportunities, consider other directions. Perhaps I would have made a great doctor. I could have moved across the river to Kentucky and been a racehorse trainer. Or I'd follow my father's footsteps and take over the family window washing business one day. Maybe I didn't keep an open mind and explore other things I enjoyed, like astronomy. I loved the sky and stars. If I hadn't been so focused on law enforcement or firefighting, would I have had a better life doing something else? I'll never know. Then again, I doubt it.

While a Graduate Assistant at the University of South Carolina, my boss was the Director of the Training Center at the Department of Corrections, which sat in the center of a huge complex dotted with prisons. I visited all of them. Remember the woman in South Carolina who was convicted of rolling her car into a lake with her two toddlers in the back seat, stating a black man stole her car with the kids in it? Well, she was in the women's prison. Murderers and rapists went to the Supermax prison, where inmates were limited to just one hour per day outside their cell. That was a dreadful place. As much as it was interesting to see firsthand how a prison operates, I was glad to work at the training center, teaching Management Development courses to Correctional Officers. The director was a retired US Secret Service Agent, and he liked me a lot. His name was Jay Lanigan, an older gentleman with silver hair. He was soft spoken but authoritative at the same time, and I'm not sure why he treated me so well. Maybe because he felt like a father figure to me as I regularly asked for career advice from him. Maybe I reminded him of his son, who was in undergrad at USC. Either way, I know he wanted me to succeed and helped me achieve my goals. I didn't realize it at the time, but Jay taught me the adage; *it's not what you know, it's who you know.* Unfortunately, I only concentrated on *what* I knew and hadn't yet begun surrounding myself with people that could help me get what I wanted. Up until then, everything that I had achieved was on my own.

One day, Jay said to me, "Alex, having a master's is great, but you need street experience. If you're interested, and when you're ready, I'll call up Sheriff Bettis and tell him I'm sending my best guy over." I later took Jay up on the offer and went in for an interview with the Sheriff. He hired me on the spot. No background investigation, no delay, no bullshit. For the first time in my life, I got something because I knew the right person.

I started the State Police Academy never having handled a gun in my life, and, eight weeks later, graduated from the Academy as the Physical Fitness Champion. I was pretty good at handling my service revolver, a Smith & Wesson .357. Standing six feet, weighing 155 pounds, I was twenty-four years old but looked like eighteen, at the most. *Officer presence* was something I needed, and fast.

I was assigned to an FTO — Field Training Officer — who was a home-grown South Carolinian, divorced, overweight, and balding. *That must suck*, I thought to myself. For another eight weeks, I trained with the deputy, day-in and day-out, riding in a marked patrol car, answering calls a police officer takes. When he'd feel I was ready to go on my own, he'd let the captain know and I'd be cut loose and on my own in my own patrol car. I was in no rush. I had a lot to learn. It's not like I didn't have the basic training or confidence to be a Sheriff's Deputy on my own, but it was my first real job, so I didn't want to screw it up. The FTO had me drive the police car, and I was getting familiar with the different areas of responsibility for each guy on the shift. I was assigned to B-shift, or *swing shift* as we called it — the 3:00 p.m. to 11:00 p.m. shift. It was the best shift to end up on, as we typically handled most calls that police officers wanted to respond to — domestic violence, bar fights, convenience store robberies, runaways, and more domestic violence. I'm not saying every shift was action-packed, there definitely were some slow days, too. Occasionally, on one of those slow days, my FTO and I would go through a drive-through fast food restaurant, and he'd say he needed to stop by his house, a double-wide in one of the many trailer parks in Lexington County. I'd stay in the marked police car and eat my burger and fries while he went inside and played video games for an hour or so, hoping he wouldn't get a *call-to-service* from the dispatcher. *It's no wonder his wife left him.* I just couldn't wrap my mind around how someone could live like that. Being at the beginning of my career, I had big dreams and expectations, and that, seeing his situation, only served to strengthen my resolve to work hard toward my goals.

One day, somehow, he got wise to the fact that an overweight, video game-addicted guy with a high school education living in a double-wide is probably behind the eight ball when it comes to finding a semi-attractive, sober, educated girl with a decent family and moral background. Not sure what brought on the change, but he stopped chewing tobacco, got a haircut, and started getting into shape. It wasn't an easy process. He had to make some serious changes, and he was doing just that; albeit taking it slow since he was in new territory, figuring out what he needed to do to make the situation work for him as opposed to remaining in a bad spot on the billiards table. *Good for him!* It's never easy to try to break away from bad habits and make a positive change. So, after my eight weeks with him were over, he cut me loose. I was on my own.

My call sign was Echo Two Zero Eight. I was given the oldest police car in the entire Sheriff's Office, a 1987 Chevy Caprice. It was one of those boxy cars you'd see on an episode of the *Andy Griffith Show*. I felt like Barney Fife driving it. It was embarrassing. Not only was I driving through Mayberry in the oldest relic in the county, but I also wasn't provided a walkie-talkie. Apparently, the Sheriff's Office didn't have enough of those. The only means of communication I had was the base radio in my Caprice. Whenever I responded to a scene, I had no way of contacting my dispatcher or other deputies after exiting my car. This was an incredibly dangerous situation, but I wasn't going to start my career complaining to the captain. Hell, I felt like I was ten feet tall and bulletproof!

I was the newest guy on the team, and there were only five of us covering a huge county, divided into five sections. Three of these sections met at a crossroads where a honky-tonk establishment was located. For those not familiar with a honky-tonk, it was a roadhouse bar frequented by the locals, mainly white, twenty-something year old guys with a lower education who were very fond of big pick-up trucks, cowboy hats, and trashy girls. It was a favorite spot after a long week working on transmissions, or on a construction site. The boys could chase the girls while there was plenty of cold Budweiser on tap, and everyone wore Wrangler blue jeans and cowboy boots. Line dancing was the go-to dance, paired with Dwight Yoakam blasting from the speakers; music spilling into the parking lot dotted with Ford F-150 pickup trucks and coolers full of Bud. Since the roadhouse was located at the crossroads, either one of the three deputies on the road working the surrounding areas could respond to a call from the dispatcher.

In the Lexington County Sheriff's Office, the first deputy to arrive on the scene became the incident commander, regardless of the rank, and oversaw the police response. If we worked Friday night, we were virtually guaranteed to receive a call-to-service to the roadhouse, called Moonshiners. When the call came in on a particular Friday not long after I started riding on my own, all three deputies responded to the dispatcher affirming their availability to respond to the scene and that they were 10-17 to the scene. *10-17* was a ten-code used in South Carolina, and in half the other states in the country, which meant *enroute to that location.* We would have entire conversations using ten-codes and signal codes over the radio. On that night, when I was working one of the three districts which could respond to the honky-tonk, my conversation with the dispatcher went something like this:

Dispatcher: "10-88, 10-83, 10-66, Moonshiners, possible 10-75, Signal 10. Also have a Signal 14 at the same location."

Translation: "Any unit in the area, there is a fight in progress and also a report of drag racing taking place at Moonshiners with a possible shooting with non-life-threating injuries as well as a complaint of indecent exposure."

Me: "Dispatch, Two Zero Eight. 10-17, Code 3."

Translation: "Dispatch, Deputy Two Zero Eight is enroute to that location using emergency lights and sirens."

Immediately after my call to the dispatcher, my two colleagues, Two Zero Four and Two Zero Seven, would respond to the dispatcher saying that they were also enroute to Moonshiners with lights and sirens. Of the three responding deputies, the first to arrive would be in command, that's how it worked. And of course, we all wanted to be the one in charge, so we would race each other to Moonshiners. I managed to arrive first.

Once I arrived on the scene: "Dispatch, Two Zero Eight, 10-23, 10-35. 10-4 the 10-83 but 10-10 the 10-66. 10-75 no injuries.

Translation: "Dispatch, Deputy Two Zero Eight. I arrived on the scene. Bar fight in progress but there is no drag racing incident. There has been a shooting with no one injured."

It was a typical Friday night at Moonshiners. Pick-up trucks and other old beaters were scattered around the parking lot. Two rednecks were fighting at the entrance to the bar, with their girlfriends trying to stop them from pounding on each other. Inside the bar, two other girls decided it was a great idea to take their tops off, hence the indecent exposure claim. It turned out that the guys who were fighting had a disagreement over the billiards game and decided to *take the disagreement outside.* They stopped dead in their tracks when the other two deputies and I calmly approached. We were known as *The*

40

Law. Once the law was present, everything tended to fall back to normal. I told the fighting guys to take a hike, so they got in their trucks and disappeared. I was more concerned with the report of a weapon being used. The bar manager explained that a regular named Travis was showing off to his friends with his new Remington 870 shotgun and fired a round into the trunk of a nearby tree. Travis was already gone by the time I arrived. We left the scene after twenty minutes or so. It was just another Friday night at the honky-tonk.

Bar scenes are not the only interesting calls local police respond to, though. Most of our calls, at least in Lexington County, were domestic disturbance matters. I was finishing up a double shift, covering a night shift for another deputy, when I received a call around 5:00 a.m. It was the third or fourth domestic I responded to that night, which isn't unusual. This call-to-service was in one of the nicest trailer parks in the county — these were citizens who had decent jobs as teachers, business managers, general contractors, and so on. A typical *domestic* usually involved a wife who called the police because her husband smacked her around. I'd arrive and be invited into the trailer to ensure the safety of the caller and to write a police report and advise the complainant of his or her rights in the matter. Once inside the trailer, I'd turn the lights on so I could assess the situation, look for the husband, and determine whether any weapons were lying about. Hitting the light switch would send all the roaches on the kitchen counter and in the sink scrambling, seeking refuge in the drain, behind an open can of soup, or in a hole in the backsplash. Answering domestics was enough to make my skin crawl. After every shift, I'd go home and shower, scrubbing the day's grime and filth off. But on this call, I didn't even make it into the trailer.

The call came in from the dispatcher: "Two Zero Eight, 10-49, Forest Glen trailer park."

"10-4, 10-17," I replied.

When I arrived at the provided address of the complainant — the wife of the accused — she explained her husband was across the street at the trailer they lived in together. She was calling from her friend's house. The woman had a nasty cut on her shin from what appeared to be a knife. I asked her if she required medical attention, but she shook her head and said she could bandage it up herself. Her husband was drunk again and the two got into an argument in their trailer. She grabbed a kitchen knife to defend herself, a struggle ensued, and she was visibly injured.

It's important to note the *visibly injured* part of my initial assessment during my conversation with this woman who called the police to help her after the argument with her husband. In South Carolina, as in many states, domestic violence calls bind the responding officer to make an arrest of a person accused of injuring another if the patrol officer sees *physical manifestations of injury* consistent with the complainant's version of what transpired. In other words, if the caller tells the police the spouse physically abused her (or him) resulting in any injury such as a bloody nose or bruised face, and the officer sees a bloody nose or bruised face, then the officer, by law, must take custody of the accused, assuming he or she is still at the location. In most domestic violence cases, it is a husband who beats his wife. And in most domestic violence cases, by the time the police arrive, the husband is no longer there. The wrong doer knows that if they are on site when *the law* shows up, someone is going to jail. It's that simple. At least this was the case in South Carolina in the mid-1990s.

"Is your husband home now?" I asked the complainant.

"Yeah, he's home. He was out late drinkin' with his buddies, so he's still awake from last night. Never went to bed, still drunk."

"Does he have any weapons in the house?"

"Uh, yeah, he's got a revolver and shotgun."

"All right. Is he alone? Any friends in there with him? Kids? Parents?"

"No, officer. He's in there alone. Dumbass is probably passed out on the couch."

The sky was getting light. I was tired as hell after working sixteen straight hours and didn't have the strength to deal with this guy's bullshit, but I had no choice. As I crossed the street, I heard Hank Williams Jr. music playing inside the trailer. Since most mobile homes were trailers on wheels, they were elevated a few feet off the ground. I walked up the wooden steps and pounded on the flimsy screen door before stepping back again, away from the front door.

"Mike, it's the Sheriff's Office. Open up."

No answer, so I repeated my demand. "Open the door, Mike. Your wife called. She's across the street."

Hank Williams stopped playing and the screen door opened a few inches. I remained in the front yard, away from the door, avoiding the *fatal funnel.* The problems with domestic violence cases are plentiful, and it doesn't matter whether the call is at a mobile home park or university professor's house in an affluent neighborhood, we never know what is behind someone's front door. The police are walking into a house without much information to go on. Granted, I knew the name of the guy there and knew he was home. I also knew that there were no warrants for his arrest. His wife told me he owned two guns, but what I didn't know is whether he had either of these weapons behind the screen door or hidden somewhere inside that he might want to use against me. Although I was told he is alone, that's not guaranteed. He was intoxicated, yes, but I didn't know if Mike was under the influence of any drugs which might have had an influence on his state of mind or his strength.

Imagine your spouse calling the police and inviting the cop into your home, accusing you of beating the crap out of him or her. If you're still there, you will probably be arrested. No one wants to be put in handcuffs and be told what to do in their own house! And this is what makes these types of calls so dangerous for the responding police officer. In this case, though, the complainant was across the street, so I was very hesitant to enter the mobile home without her inside. In most cases, the police have no right to walk into someone's home uninvited. If she was home and invited me in, then I would have the right to enter, but she was across the street. In this situation, it was a legal gray area. Mike certainly wasn't going to ask me to come inside, so my best course of action was to get him out of the trailer and into the front yard, away from any weapons he likely had access to. If I could get him outside, it would be safer for me to deal with him one-on-one. Since his wife was visibly injured and claimed that Mike cut her leg with a knife, not only could I arrest him, but by law, I was obligated. But how was I going to do that? What sort of Jedi mind-trick could I use to lure him out into the front yard? My mind was racing, and I thought about the training I received at the South Carolina Police Academy.

"Mike, come outside a sec."

"I ain't comin' out."

"Mike, I just spoke with your wife. She's cut bad. We'll get her patched up, but I just need to get a statement from you for my report."

"I come outside, you're gonna arrest me."

Yeah, Mike knew the law. He knew that I had the legal authority I needed to put him in handcuffs. They usually do.

"No, sir. I will not arrest you," I lied. "I am finishing my shift and want to take care of this quickly. I would rather talk to you quietly as opposed to shouting through the door. You really want your neighbors to hear us talking?"

A pause. "You're not going to arrest me?"

"No, why would I arrest you?"

"Because we had a fight."

"Yes, I know. But look, Mike, I already wrote a police report for your wife," I lied again, "and she said you cut her with a knife. She is indeed injured, and it appears that the contusion is from a fixed blade of some sort. If she wants to, she can go to the Magistrate's office today with that police report and press charges against you for domestic violence. She has the right to do that, Mike," I continued from the front lawn while he was still inside. "If she does that, the next shift will come back here later today and arrest you. What I suggest is I write a report for you — *your* side of the story — and then you can take it to the Magistrate's office first thing in the morning before she gets there, and *you* get a warrant for *her* arrest."

Mike didn't say anything, and I wasn't sure if my ruse was working.

"Mike, I'm going to my car to write the report for you. Come out to give me the details."

As I turned my back on Mike and his double wide, I walked across his lawn to my marked patrol car in the street. Keeping my pace casual, I sensed that he was following me, surprised a bit that he was dumb enough to fall for the bullshit I was putting out. Once by the car, I spotted Mike's reflection in the patrol car windows and saw that he was wearing cut-off jean shorts and *wifebeater,* a white tank top. He was slim, had a few tattoos, and would be no match for me should he decide to resist being arrested. Had I been turned to him, he would have noticed the small smile forming on my face.

I opened my rear car door and tossed my clipboard on the back seat. As I turned around, all serious again, to face him in the middle of the street, I demanded, "Put your hands on the trunk of my car. You're under arrest for domestic violence."

"You motherfucker!" he yelled as I patted him down and put him in the back of my patrol car, cuffed in handcuffs! "Fuck you, Doogie Howser son of a bitch!"

Great. So, my young appearance warranted me a nickname *Doogie Howser* based on a 1980s sitcom featuring Neil Patrick Harris as a child prodigy doctor. I guess I could have been offended, but I thought it was funny that my *rookie looks* worked in my favor to help outsmart this guy.

* * *

Another odd encounter I had as a Sheriff's Deputy was when I got a call from the dispatcher that a woman had been kidnapped but managed to get to a phone to call 911. Dispatch had the woman on the phone while providing me with the address and the details. The caller was at a pay phone in the middle of nowhere in the western part of the county, in an area without many houses. The pay phone was in a gravel parking lot of a local sandwich shop, which was now closed since it was around 10:00 p.m. Driving close to hundred miles per hour, it didn't take me long to get there. It was dark outside, but the lot was well lit. As I approached the area, slowing down to a manageable speed, I noticed the pay phone and spotted the woman inside the phone booth. There was a car parked next to it with a male in the driver's seat. Dispatch and

I were communicating regularly during my response to the parking lot, and I was told that the woman is in the phone booth and her kidnapper was in the car waiting for her.

What the fuck? So, you're telling me this woman was kidnapped and asked her kidnapper to let her use the payphone while he waited in the car? Something was off.

"Two Zero Eight," said the dispatcher as I rolled toward the parking lot, "Complainant states the kidnapper has a gun."

Ok, this escalated quickly.

With my emergency lights cutting through the darkness of the night, I slid into the gravel lot sideways, coming to a stop twenty feet or so behind the assailant's vehicle. Next to the suspect's vehicle was the phone booth, woman inside, talking with my dispatcher. I opened the door of my patrol car and positioned myself in the wedge of the opened door. Hunched down to take cover, I withdrew my Smith & Wesson .357 Magnum revolver, and pointed it at the occupant in the driver's seat of the vehicle next to the phone booth.

"Ma'am, put the phone down and step away from the phone booth. Circle around toward your right, come around me, and get into the back seat of my patrol car," I stated loud enough for the woman to hear my voice over the hum of my car engine.

"But I'm on the phone with the police," she answered.

"Ma'am, I am the police. I'm talking to the same person you are talking to on the phone. Put the phone down and circle to your right, come back toward the sound of my voice, and get into the back of my vehicle."

As the caller did what she was told, I relayed the vehicle's tag number for the dispatcher to run the tags to find out who the car was registered to, their address, and whether there were any warrants for the owner's arrest. Dispatch responded ten seconds later with the name and address of the vehicle owner. He had no active arrest warrants, so that was good news. A deputy who was patrolling the next section of the county was listening to my conversation with the dispatcher and was on the way, lights and sirens wailing.

Once the complainant reached my car, I put her in the back seat and told her to sit tight. Meanwhile, the man in the car seemed upset, repeatedly yelling, trying to determine why the police arrived.

"Sir, please calm down, turn your engine off, and show me your hands." He complied, sticking both hands out the driver's side window, which was down. "With your left hand, open the door from the outside." Again, the driver did what he was told. I proceeded to go through all the commands police officers are trained to give during a high-risk vehicle stop — get out of the car and face away from the sound of my voice; slowly raise your shirt with one hand so I can see your waistline while the other hand is raised above your head and turn clock-wise until I tell you to stop; with both your hands raised above your head, slowly walk backwards to the sound of my voice; stop; get down on your right knee; get down on both knees; put your hands on the ground in front of you; lay down on the ground and face to the right; spread your feet; keep your arms out to your side; turn your thumbs toward your feet; don't move.

By the time I went through all the directions and the male complied, Echo Two Zero Seven was rolling into the parking lot. Once Two Zero Seven stopped his patrol car, he popped out of his vehicle and drew his pistol, backing me up so I could handcuff the suspect.

I quickly put my handcuffs on the guy while he was laying prone on the gravel parking lot and got him to his feet after a thorough search for weapons.

"Brian, can you check his vehicle for weapons or contraband?" I asked the other deputy. With Two Zero Seven on the scene, I had a chance to interview the female caller who had contacted the dispatcher about being kidnapped.

As it turned out, the caller — the person who claimed to be kidnapped by a man with a gun — was not being kidnapped at all. She had met the guy at a bar that night, agreed to go back to his house with him for some fun, got cold feet on the way to his house and asked him to stop at a pay phone so she could call her babysitter to let her know that she would be home later than planned. The babysitter story was a

47

lie, but it got her out of the vehicle. The call to the police was simply a way out and to get away from the guy without telling him that he was no longer going to get lucky that night, which she feared may upset him and put her in a dangerous situation. She lied to the dispatcher and pulled two deputies off the street because she changed her mind about letting some random guy from a bar take her back to his house to get laid. *You've got to be kidding me.*

I interviewed him next, and his story matched hers. He was at a nearby bar enjoying a beer while playing pool. The girl had a couple too many (drinks) and was showing her cleavage. He struck up a conversation with her, eventually suggesting they go back to his trailer for more fun. She agreed and got into his car but then asked him to stop at the pay phone so she could call her babysitter. Next thing he knows; my police car spotlight and blue emergency lights were blinding him through the rear glass of his faded 1989 Mercury Cougar, and he heard my voice. He thought he was getting lucky, and instead, found himself cuffed on the ground in a vacant parking lot next to broken beer bottles.

I took the cuffs off the guy, who I never arrested but put the bracelets on him for his safety (and mine) while I could sort through the events of the evening. It definitely was not a good night for this poor guy! Instead of getting laid, he was being detained by a young Deputy Sheriff in a *Smokey the Bear* hat who looked like *Doogie Howser.* I let him go. As for the young lady who filed a false police report, I sure as hell could have charged her, but I wasn't about to. I gave her a ride back to her apartment, politely advising her to be a bit more cautious about being picked up in a bar and going home with random men. Funny thing was she was older than me, but I was the one giving her advice. Another shift, another story to tell.

Living in Columbia, South Carolina, had run its course. I loved going to college there, and I loved being a police officer, but it was just too small of a town. I realized it was time to move on after making a stop at Wendy's restaurant one night at a truck stop somewhere along Interstate 26, which stretched from Charleston to Greenville. I remember it like it was yesterday and will never forget it. I just happened to be working another graveyard shift, and I walked up to the counter to place my order. As I turned to find a place to sit and eat my sandwich, a mother and boy were seated nearby, eating their dinner, although it was 2:00 a.m. I wondered what they were doing there in the middle of the night. Maybe they were passing through, on the way to the mountains for a camping trip. Or maybe they were fleeing an abusive husband and father. I'm not sure, but both stared at me as I sat down, unwrapped a cheeseburger, and let my dispatcher know that I was busy eating dinner.

"Dispatch, Two Zero Eight. 10-6."

"10-4, Two Zero Eight."

It was as if I was a creature from Mars to that mother and child. Dressed in my uniform, revolver visible, radio squawking occasionally, my Smokey the Bear hat on the table. The kid couldn't take his eyes off me. I wondered what his thoughts were, and I knew then and there that I didn't want to do this for the rest of my career. It was my dream job, but as it happens, dreams change. They grow and morph as we are being shaped by our life experiences. I stayed with the Sheriff's Office for another year before I joined the US Border Patrol.

3
The Green Machine

I was done with South Carolina and needed something bigger. Don't take me wrong, my time at the Sheriff's Office was everything I was hoping for and to this day, I fondly remember those early years of my career. But once I reached that goal, I wanted more. I was hungry for more adventure and dared myself to dream bigger. US Border Patrol sounded exciting and the idea of becoming a federal agent was very appealing, so, I gave it a try and applied. After a series of interviews and, once my background investigation was finished, I was offered a position as a Border Patrol Agent.

When I accepted the offer to be a Border Patrol Agent, I didn't know where I'd be assigned, but I assumed it would be on our southern border with Mexico. It didn't really matter to me, to be honest. Texas would be fine, and Arizona would be great, yet I was really hoping to get assigned to San Diego. I got lucky and was posted to the Brown Field Station, along the Tijuana border just south of San Diego. In fact, my entire training academy class was assigned to the San Diego Sector. This was in the mid-90s when the Justice Department was hiring just about everyone who applied to the Border Patrol.

I started my six months of training at the Federal Law Enforcement Training Center along the southeast coast of Georgia in a small port city called Brunswick. The training center is a massive facility, utilized by several federal law enforcement agencies to train recruits in defensive tactics, firearms, high-speed driving, handcuffing techniques, and law.

The Border Patrol Academy is widely known as one of the toughest federal academies to complete. Not only was the physical training very demanding, but we also needed to learn to speak Spanish, pass firearms training, driver training and immigration law. Spanish, for me, was relatively simple since I had taken a few years of it during grade school, and high school. The fitness aspect of it was demanding but a lot of fun, and easy since I kept in shape, but it was learning the immigration law that turned out to be brutal. As a student in the Border Patrol Academy, we couldn't fail any test during the six-month training period. If we failed a single written test, we were sent home. We'd lose our jobs, on the spot. To say there was a bit of a pressure at the academy is an understatement. None of us failed any tests, but I, and few others, came close a couple of times. If we passed though, no one cared about the score. We were just glad to make it through each law exam without losing a classmate.

Attending a police academy is a lot like attending college. You learn about your tradecraft, yes, but you learn a lot about yourself and your colleagues. We trained together, studied together, ate breakfast, lunch, and dinner together. On most weekends, we'd drive across the causeway onto Saint Simons Island, a picturesque barrier island on the Atlantic Ocean, and get a few beers at Brogen's Pub. We grew close and developed friendships that would last a lifetime. I didn't know it then, of course, but after retiring, I moved to Saint Simons Island to enjoy the serenity of the marshes and Live Oak trees draped in Spanish Moss, the challenging golf courses, and the magnificent beach on nearby Sea Island. But as I mentioned earlier, we don't really know what's going on behind someone's front door. Years later, one of the members of Class 314 sent out an email to our class congratulating everyone on our ten-year graduation anniversary and informed the rest of us that another classmate known as Mongo had recently taken his own life. What a shame! I was very close to Mongo when we were in training together and after we began working in San Diego, but I lost touch with him after I left the Border Patrol, and we were never in contact again. My heart ached for him and his family, and I never knew that life had gotten to that point for him.

After six months of training, we all graduated. I took home the Physical Fitness Champion honors and was very proud about that, but it wasn't over yet, there was still one last obstacle to overcome. Spanish language training continued for another three months after we graduated. One day each week, the entire class — all twenty-four of us — were required to attend a full day of language class at a linguist school outside of San Diego. At the end of three months, we would take our final oral exam to demonstrate our mastery of the Spanish language. If we failed that test, we'd lose our job and be sent home. Again, no pressure, right? We were still not in the clear.

By this time, after nine months of intensive language training and having to speak Spanish during every shift with the people we'd arrest, most of us became fluent Spanish speakers. A colleague of ours struggled with it, though. One by one, we'd take our final oral exam, which took maybe fifteen minutes each. Those that passed the test came out of the testing center with a big smile and high-fives. *"Excellente, hermano!"* we'd say as each of us passed the test. We were finally finished with training! But then, Big Mike came out after his oral exam. He told us he failed by three points and was informed by the board examiners he was no longer employed and should leave the premises immediately. "Go back to the station and turn in your weapon, Mr. Mitchell," the lead examiner told him. Big Mike was absolutely devastated and the rest of us were shocked. After training together for nine months, and getting to know each other, it was horrible to see Mike leave us. He called his wife to break the news and drove away. The rest of us looked at each other in disbelief and, for those who still had to take the exam, the stress level went through the roof.

Suddenly, the lead examiner came out of the testing center, looking around. "Where's Mr. Mitchell?" he asked.

"He left, sir. He's gone."

"Does anyone have his number?"

Someone gave the examiner Big Mike's cell phone number, and the examiner called him.

"Mr. Mitchell, I'm so sorry. We made a mistake with scoring your test. You passed."

And just like that, Big Mike was a Patrol Agent once again. A graduate of Class 314.

Crazy mistakes happen all the time, but at least this time, they realized it almost immediately; no real harm was done. Mike kept his job and was one of us again.

After graduation, all new recruits were teamed up with Field Training Officers to learn how migrants enter the United States without being detected by *La Migra*, or Immigration Officers. My call sign was Bravo One Six Four. We arrested dozens of suspected illegal immigrants crossing the US/Mexico border every night. It was a great job, but the reality was these lawbreakers were not a high priority for the US Department of Justice. The US Attorney's Office in San Diego very rarely prosecuted the migrants. Sure, every single person we arrested would have been convicted in federal court if the Attorney's Office accepted our cases for prosecution, but these cases weren't sexy enough for the prosecutors. They didn't want to waste their time with illegal immigrants who were simply coming to the US for the seasonal work so they could send money home to support their families, wherever that might be. The prosecutors wanted the bigger fish. They wanted to nail murderers and drug dealers, not poor Mexicans, or Guatemalans. I can't blame them. We would make the arrests, process them in jail, then put them on a bus to take them back to the Tijuana border where they would be let free to go back into Mexico. Think they were deterred by being arrested? No, not at all. They'd only come back, again and again, until they made it past us. It was a bit frustrating to work hard to make these arrests, only to be undermined by the prosecutors. But whatever, it was a fun job and it paid well. That's all I really cared about.

After a few months of working along the Southern border, we were good at tracking migrants entering the United States from Mexico. Along the US/Mexico border, at least in California, foot trails leading from Mexico into the *land of opportunity* are plentiful. They are numbered and Border Patrol Agents know these trails well. Among them are seismic sensors — boxes about the size of a shoebox, buried just below the surface. A thin antenna is connected to the box and sticks out of the ground twelve inches or so and is virtually invisible, hiding in plain sight amongst the chaparral covering the ground. Whenever there is a movement on the surface, such as an animal or person walking nearby, the ground shakes ever-so-slightly, alerting the sensor of the disruption to the dirt around it. The sensor relays this information to the dispatcher who, in turn, calls out to the Border Patrol Agents in the area to inform them that someone or something just walked past the sensor. Most of the time, migrants head north toward Chula Vista, one of the neighborhoods in San Diego closest to Mexico. An agent or two patrolling the trail area just north of where the sensor was buried would wait alongside the trail to intercept those migrants and arrest them. Thinking they were hidden under the blanket of the dark night; the migrants unknowingly walk right into a Border Patrol ambush.

"All units near Otay Lakes, the 1875 just took two hits," the dispatcher said in a tone that was both calm and routine one night when I was working the Otay Lakes area about a mile north of Mexico. I jumped on it.

"Dispatch, Bravo One Six Four, 10-17 to the 1875."

"Roger, One Six Four. Anyone else in the area?" the dispatcher called over the radio. "One Six Four will need some backup. The 1875 just took two more hits."

No one responded. No one was available to help me, and the 1875 sensor has just taken four hits which meant this was a group of twelve or maybe fifteen people. I was just hoping the group wasn't being led by a human smuggler, aptly nicknamed *Coyote*. The *coyotes* are usually Mexican men who are paid by anyone wanting safe passage into the United States. Coyotes sell their craft to central and south Americans on the streets of Tijuana and other cities in Mexico for hundreds, sometime even thousands, of dollars. They collect the money under a promise of a guaranteed arrival at a safe house in the San Diego area, or maybe Los Angeles. But you see, since they've been pre-paid for leading their customers on a dangerous trek over the Otay Mountains just south of San Diego, their loyalty only goes so far. Coyotes will abandon their travelers, desperate enough to pay big chunks of their savings to come across, at the first hint of a Border Patrol Agent and flee, adeptly evading the agents. They know the trails and the terrain as well as we do, and they know where some of the seismic sensors are located, so they avoid certain trails. They're very good at what they do.

Dressed in my olive-green Border Patrol uniform and black Danner boots, I was carrying a Camelback hydration system, a couple Streamlight rechargeable flashlights, Motorola radio, and Beretta 96D Brigadier 40-caliber pistol. I parked my green and white US Border Patrol Ford Bronco along Otay Lakes Boulevard, a deserted stretch of road in an area heavily patrolled by Patrol Agents. Once the SUV was locked, I made my way into the darkness, heading on a dirt footpath south toward the 1875 sensor on the only trail leading north from where the sensor was buried.

Patience and stealth. That's what it took to find some of these groups. As I crouched near the 1875 trail, positive that the group was coming my way, I listened.

"One Six Four, we're headed your way. What's your Twenty?" I could hear another agent calling over the radio. I replied with my 10-20, or location, but since I was too far back into a canyon, my radio call didn't make it to the other agents. In the mountains, this wasn't unusual. Sometimes you can hear others on the radio, and sometimes you can't. It just depended on where you were located and how far away the repeater antenna was located.

Fifteen minutes later, "One Six Four, in the blind, we found your Bronco and are coming toward you on the 1875. Four PAs headed your way, ten minutes out."

I replied again but I still couldn't reach the others.

As the group of migrants approached my position from the south, I could hear them whispering in Spanish. *"¿Dónde coño estamos?"* one would say. *"¿Dónde estamos? ¿Dónde está la Inmigración? Esa es la pregunta que debemos hacer?"* another would reply. It was obvious they didn't know where they were and, more importantly, were not aware of my presence, or that I was ready to take them down. As they got closer to my position, I counted twelve or thirteen people, likely Honduran nationals, but it was difficult to be certain, even with the full moon glowing over the valley and desert grasses. *How was I going to round up all these migrants by myself?* I had to outsmart them. *Alright, let's play a ruse... Stay low, speak Spanish, and get them on the ground,* I thought to myself. As the group crept quietly through the dark along the trail headed to safety and freedom of Los Angeles, I stood up, planting myself in the middle of the dirt trail in front of them and whispered, *"Sientate, no se muevan."* I continued speaking in Spanish, "Sit down and don't move. I'm a Border Patrol Agent. If you do what I tell you to do, the *chupacabra* will stay away and you might be able to return to Mexico tonight," referring to a Latin mythical creature resembling a goat or wild dog that could fly and was believed to prey on small animals and, at times, worked with the Border Patrol to arrest and even kill illegal aliens traveling north. Most illegals, Hondurans included, were scared as hell of the mythical chupacabra and would do exactly what they're told. I tried to use my radio again to let the dispatcher know I apprehended twelve people and to relay my location, but no one could hear me. I was still too deep ino the canyon. *Thank goodness it wasn't a group led by a coyote, just some naïve and harmless migrants taking a chance. It could have been bad news.* Just then, I heard the whir of a helicopter buzz in from the north.

"One Six Four, this is Foxtrot. What's your 10-20?" the helicopter patrol officer said calmly over the Motorola.

"Good timing, Fox, thanks for the help." I looked up in the sky and heard the rotors whipping the air but didn't see the Border Patrol *helo* against the jet-black sky. "One hundred meters north of the 1875, four hundred meters south of Dolzura bridge."

Because he had patrolled this area for the last ten years, the pilot new exactly where I was, turned on his powerful spotlight directed toward the ground, and pointed the helicopter in my direction, canvassing the 1875 trail south from the bridge to where I was located with a group of suspected illegal immigrants. The *helo* was twenty-five feet off the ground and lit the surrounding area with blinding light, scattering dried reeds, small trees bending under the mighty gusts of the winds. He stopped right over us and hovered, scaring the hell out of the

Hondurans. As I put flexicuffs on each of the weary migrants with the help of the light from the helicopter and started walking them out of the ravine toward my Bronco, I finally heard a voice come over my radio and was relieved to have contact with the other agents on the ground.

"One Six Four, do you copy?"

"10-4. Lima Charlie." I copy, loud and clear.

"What's your status?"

"10-15 times twelve. 10-13, 10-45," I replied. "Twelve aliens apprehended. I'm coming to you with all twelve."

"10-4, One Six Four. Dispatch, Bravo One Six Four is 10-15 times twelve. Send a 10-16," the other agent replied, relaying the message to the dispatcher. "Agent Reinshagen arrested twelve migrants, unassisted, on the 1875 hit. Send transport to come get these people."

"Nice work, One Six Four!" the dispatcher replied.

Foxtrot extinguished his lights and disappeared north, likely to help another agent arrest another group. It never ended. There were always plenty of stories like this one to go around. For me, it was just another routine night on the Southwest border.

"Thanks, again, for the help, Foxtrot."

* * *

Each night, one agent was assigned an overwatch position from atop a mountain which overlooked the Otay Mesa port of entry, the busiest semi-trailer border crossing in the world. From the top of this mountain, one could see the Pacific Ocean to the west, the city of San Diego to the north, and Tijuana, Mexico, to the south. After dark, the overwatch agent used an infrared camera to search the mesa, or flat land below the mountain, for warm bodies. The agent operating the huge infrared camera was responsible for spotting groups of suspected migrants attempting to get into the United States from the south. The telescope's infrared light would detect objects emitting some form of electromagnetic radiation, or simply put, heat. This device gave us a huge advantage, even more so since the migrants didn't know it existed. But it didn't always detect humans. Sometimes the agent would see images he believed to be bodies walking north and Border Patrol

57

Agents would be sent to intercept the migrants, and make arrests, only to come up empty.

"Bravo One Six Four, we've got a group of eight headed your way, up the 1425 trail. They're five minutes away," the overwatch agent would say after spotting a group of warm bodies making their way north about three miles from his location on the top of the mountain. A few minutes later, I'd see some movement south of my position and hunker down along the 1425 trail, expecting to arrest eight migrants. No such luck! Sometimes, what overwatch thought they saw and what they *really* saw wasn't the same.

"Cattle, overwatch. They're cows."

"Sorry, One Six Four. They looked like Guatemalans from here."

Well, it was never a dull moment nor a dull shift being a Border Patrol Agent. It was great work, and I loved being in the action. But my personal and social life suffered. When I first moved to San Diego and started working as an agent, I decided to rent a studio apartment in the downtown area. The nightlife was great and there were plenty of restaurants conveniently located within walking distance, but it was expensive. Most of my Border Patrol Academy classmates lived south of the city near Imperial Beach with roommates to offset the high costs of living in Southern California. But having a roommate didn't appeal to me, and neither did living so close to the Mexican border. After a year of struggling to pay my bills while living in the Gaslamp Quarter, I decided to look for a new place to live. Having a roommate to split the rent made good financial sense, and I was lucky to find a guy who needed a roommate in Pacific Beach, just a few blocks from the ocean, and I moved in. We got along great. Rent was cheap, I was living by the beach, running every day. I was tan, single and twenty-five years old. I was living a dream. If only I had time to enjoy it. Working long hours, weekends, and nights complicated things. And although I had plenty of opportunities to meet girls in our circle, I didn't have the time for it, and couldn't even imagine raising a family with this work schedule. *Hell, I was twenty-five. Should I really be worried about that at this point in my life? Or should I just enjoy the good times while I can. I* wasn't ready to have a family just yet, but I couldn't help starting to feel this wasn't *it.* Ultimately, I decided to get out of law enforcement to see what life was like Monday through Friday and test my theory of whether being pre-dispositioned into a life of law enforcement was a good thing. I was determined to have an open mind and explore other avenues.

A friend of mine from Chicago came to visit me in San Diego. I took a couple of days off work so I could spend time with him while he was in town. We drove into Mexico about an hour south and had a few beers on Rosarito Beach in Baja. Kevin was an outside salesman for a construction supply company in Chicago and made a lot more money than I, for what sounded like easy work. He said they had an opening in St. Louis, and that he could help me get the job. I took the job and left law enforcement, and I moved out of San Diego a couple months later. Making more money, driving a company car, and having nights and weekends off was great, for a while. After six months or so of being on my own in the sales industry, still making great money, my buddy Alan, a classmate from the University of South Carolina, called me up one day.

"Alex, I know the Border Patrol wasn't doing it for you, and sales in St. Louis might be where you should be, but DSS is hiring. You should consider it!"

Alan had joined the State Department a few years back and loved it. After being out of law enforcement for the past six months, I was ready to get back in the game and decided to apply. Getting hired into federal law enforcement, and even local law enforcement for that matter, was a slow and intensive process. By intensive, I mean to say that there is a ton of paperwork to complete, forms to sign, and tests to pass. This process takes months or even years. A physical exam and physical fitness test must be passed and completed as well as drug tests, psychological tests, and a thorough background investigation is carried out to determine suitability to hold a security clearance. It seemed like there was no end to it. Finally, after two years, I was invited to participate in the final step of the selection process — a three-person panel interview with a writing skills assessment to be held in two weeks in Chicago. Excited that I was still being considered for the position, I drove the four hours from St. Louis to Chicago with high hopes to pass the last two hurdles.

Being a good writer, I crushed the written test but still had the oral part to pass. It was a conversational interview and at first, I thought I failed miserably. As the panel concluded their questions, an uneasy feeling started to grow in the pit of my stomach. It wasn't that I froze in there, nothing like that, I just didn't think it was what they were looking for. I was asked to wait in the lobby while the panel discussed my answers and decided my fate. I left the interview room and sunk into a seat in the lobby, sulking. *No way I passed*, I thought to myself. *Maybe I should just get up and walk the hell out of here and go back to St. Louis.* Just then, the door opened, and I was invited back into the interview room for the verdict.

"Mr. Reinshagen, all three of us deliberated about whether you are a good fit for the State Department, and we all agree that you are. Hopefully we can get you into the academy soon. Good luck with your new career."

Holy hell, how did I pass? I couldn't believe it, but I made it! That was one of the best days of my life, which was about to change dramatically! Six months later, I started the academy. It was September 25, 2000.

I wasn't the only one to leave the Green Machine, though. Several of us decided to take a different path, including a former lawyer who we aptly nicknamed *El Abogado*. After ten years in the Border Patrol, El Abogado transitioned to the Immigration and Customs Enforcement agency as a Special Agent. I had already moved into the Diplomatic Security Service and had been with DSS for four or five years when our paths nearly crossed again, this time in Islamabad, Pakistan. I was sent to Islamabad from my first overseas posting in Thailand to assist the Regional Security Officer there with security around the American Embassy and to protect the US Ambassador to Pakistan at that time, Nancy Powell. US General Tommy Franks had flown into Pakistan to meet with her.

In the early 2000s, the embassy compound was quite small, but it was roomy enough to have apartments for temporary duty personnel like me to live on the compound during my short assignment. I was assigned a big apartment by myself. I remember this apartment distinctly, because I mentioned to the RSO that it was a comfortable place to stay in such an inhospitable environment. The RSO agreed that the apartments are nice, but mentioned there was an *incident* last year in one of them.

"What type of incident?"

"An ICE Agent was assigned here and was scheduled to depart post one afternoon but never showed up at motor pool to catch a ride to the airport. The facilities manager knocked on the agent's apartment door to tell him he needed to get rolling, but no one answered. The FM had keys to the apartment, and after several more attempts of knocking and calling through the closed apartment door, he let himself in. He found the agent, that's for sure. Unfortunately, it was too late for him. The ICE Agent had taken his own life and was found in the bathtub after a nine-millimeter round ended his day. Lights out."

It turns out that the ICE Agent was my friend, El Abogado. From what I heard; he was going through a nasty divorce, and I guess he didn't want to return to the U.S. and face that reality. It was really sad. He was a smart guy. Funny, friendly. I still remember how much it resonated with me. I imagined something got to him and he broke. What I couldn't imagine was life being so difficult that you don't want to continue living, breathing, being a father or husband, enjoying the sunshine or anything you like doing. As I mentioned, we never know what's going on behind someone's front door. I always considered myself lucky and it was moments like these when I thanked the universe for dealing me the cards I got. Did I work hard for everything I ever achieved? Yes, of course. But it never hurts to have some luck on your side. Luck is definitely underrated.

Top US military commander, General Tommy Franks, flanked by the US Ambassador to Pakistan Nancy Powell, DSS Special Agent Alex Reinshagen, and Pakistan Army commander Lieutenant General Khateer Hassan Khan leave the Chaklala military air base in Rawalpindi, Pakistan, 2003. Photo courtesy of Getty Images.

4

The Foreign Circus

As mentioned earlier, I was born and raised in Cincinnati with core mid-western values; hard work, modesty, friendliness, and doing the right thing. Home to Procter & Gamble, Graeter's Ice Cream, the Hudepohl Brewing Company, and Skyline Chili, Cincinnati is a place most people never leave. Generation after generation are born there and make a nice living for themselves, enjoying Reds baseball games in the summer and Bengals football during the fall. Growing up in the Queen City, I remember when the famous rock band *The Who* played a concert at the Riverfront Coliseum in 1979. Back then, there were no assigned seats when you bought tickets to a concert. After the gates opened, eleven people were trampled to death trying to get to the front row. After this tragedy, assigned seating became the norm at rock concerts. I also remember that I went to high school with Pete Rose Jr. and was at Riverfront Stadium to see his father pass Ty Cobb's hit record of 4,256 career hits in 1985 against the San Diego Padres. When I was in high school, a friend and I would drive across the Ohio River to River Downs Racetrack in Kentucky and bet on the horse races. It was a safe place to grow up in the 70s and 80s. And, to this day, is an inexpensive and safe place to raise a family.

Settled by German immigrants as a meat-packing port on the Ohio River, my grandmother immigrated to Cincinnati from Germany in 1906. As the youngest of ten kids, all blonde haired, and blue eyed, I grew up being the *little brother* of all my siblings. Everyone on the west side knew the Reinshagen family, making it an easy childhood. People, even those I didn't know, looked out for me. If I needed a ride home from little league baseball practice at the local park, one of my siblings' friends would offer me a ride. People took care of each other.

So why leave? A sense of adventure, perhaps? Meeting new people and traveling to far-off places appealed to me as a child. It still does. I could easily get lost in Cambodia and be perfectly happy. Or disappear in Seoul, eating new foods and learning a new language. I've always had the urge to go somewhere and do something that seemed far-fetched from the township where I was raised, and I hated the idea of being stagnant. I enjoyed the excitement of getting away from family and friends, experiencing life beyond the Midwest, hence my decision to attend graduate school in South Carolina, work for the US Border Patrol in California, and eventually, move around the world with the US Government.

The United States Foreign Service, part of the US Department of State, is dedicated to living and working overseas at US Embassies and Consulates, promoting the President's foreign policy agenda. As a Special Agent in the US Foreign Service, I worked in the Diplomatic Security Service — the law enforcement arm of the State Department, both domestically and abroad.

The selection process to become an agent with the Diplomatic Security Service is intimidating, to say the least. The State Department in general, and specifically the US Foreign Service, prides itself in being a diverse workforce. By diverse, I'm not just referring to skin color. It's also about background and experiences, education, specialties or licenses, and communication skills. Foreign Service employees are career officers assigned around the world promoting US interests in countries where the United States has diplomatic ties. This includes over three hundred countries and entities with which the United States has a mutually beneficial relationship. An American Ambassador can be either appointed by the sitting US President or be a career diplomat, and land a particular assignment based on experience, expertise in a certain region or country, language capabilities, and so on. They represent the US in the country they are assigned to and are designated as the head of the Embassy.

An ambassador is the highest-ranking diplomat in a country in which the United State has a diplomatic relationship with that country. The

Ambassador works at the American Embassy which is in the capital of the foreign country. Several large countries have more than one American diplomatic office with the smaller of the two located in other major cities. This smaller office is called a Consulate. The highest-ranking diplomat at the Consulate holds the title of Consul General.

Diplomatic Security Service Special Agents are specialists in the security field and, as federal agents, have full arrest authority in the United States. They are assigned to field offices across the US, but are also stationed abroad as diplomats, promoting the President's foreign policies, answering to the American Ambassador, or Consul General.

Of the thousands of applicants who meet the minimum requirements to become a DSS Special Agent, less than one half of one percent are hired. Those applicants fortunate to score high enough on the written and oral exams are rank-ordered and put on a list. If you're lucky to get on the list, the US Congress must approve of funds to bring these candidates on as full-time employees. Not everyone who is offered a conditional offer of employment makes it into the Academy. Each academy class is usually twenty-four students, the cutoff number being strictly set. So, if you find yourself ranked number twenty-five on the list, you didn't make the cut and must wait another year or two before the next academy class begins. The selection criteria are so stringent, and the acceptance rate so narrow, I had a better chance of being admitted into Harvard Law School than I did of becoming a Special Agent in the US Foreign Service. The hiring process was stressful as hell, but I wouldn't trade it for anything. It took me nearly three years to get hired by DSS because, in part, the selection process involves a full background investigation, which takes more than a year to complete.

I was interviewed at the DSS Chicago Field Office by a board of three Special Agents called a Board of Examiners. For each candidate offered a career in the State Department, the BEX is making a five-million-dollar commitment. This means Congress is assuming the government will spend this amount of money on each employee throughout a normal twenty-year career. This isn't to suggest the salary of Foreign Service employees is four hundred thousand dollars per year; this figure represents a salary, health benefits, moving expenses, housing costs, overseas schooling, travel expenses, and a pension. If you're lucky enough to get hired — and luck has a lot to do with it — you're in for a hell of a career. If you survive!

* * *

At the academy, my classmates and I became a tight-knit group. Our class wasn't as diverse as the incoming classes today since, two decades ago, a diverse workforce was not a hot-ticket conversation like it is now. Of the twenty-four in my class, only three were female recruits, and only a handful were people of color. The rest were white males with military or police experience. So much for diversity back then. It is *very* different now.

We were known as Basic Special Agent Class 57, and, frankly, I was intimidated by many of them, at first. These folks had great experiences; we had a former FBI Agent in our class as well as a few former US Marines, Navy helicopter pilot, a Special Forces Chief Warrant Officer, Immigration Officer, and a lot of guys with military and police backgrounds.

Despite all the competition, I was elected the class president. It was more of a hassle than anything else at the time, but the title stood with me throughout my career. Nine months of training — protecting important people, conducting federal investigations, high-speed and off-road driving training, weapons training, defensive tactics, serving arrest warrants and search warrants as well as interviewing suspects, testifying in federal court, interviewing techniques, and report writing, the course was intense to say the least. We all got through the training and learned how to be investigators and protection specialists, but no one taught us exactly how to be an American diplomat. Our time would come.

My first assignment after completing basic training was at the Washington Field Office. When DSS Agents are assigned to a field office in the United States, one of their responsibilities is conducting federal investigations related to passport and visa fraud.

Let me try to unpack this concept. An American passport is proof of US citizenship. When someone applies for a United States passport and there is a reason to believe that the applicant is either not a United States citizen or is a citizen but is not the person listed on the application, the DSS investigates this matter to determine whether the applicant is authorized to be issued that passport. There are a few reasons why an American citizen would apply for a US passport in the identity of someone else, but it usually boils down to this — the true person doesn't want to be found. This may be because there is a warrant for the arrest of the actual person, or perhaps the applicant owes a debt or alimony they cannot or don't want to pay, so they steal another person's identity.

Another element of investigations DSS Agents conduct is US Visa Fraud. Prior to entering the United States, foreigners from certain countries must apply for a travel visa to the US at one of the hundreds of embassies and consulates overseas.

Many of these applicants submit falsified documents with their visa application to the State Department, and it's the job of a US Foreign Service Consular Officer to identify these potentially false or fake documents. If the officer suspects this is the case, then the investigations are assigned to a DSS Agent to investigate the matter and establish whether the applicant is truthful and should be granted a travel visa to enter the United States.

Conducting investigations is not a job that is coveted by most DSS Agents. Personally, I loved the investigations, but I was in the minority. Most agents liked working protective security operations. I'm sure you've seen plenty of movies involving agents in suits with an earpiece tucked in their ear, protecting a VIP. Just like there is no shortage of films depicting an attack on a motorcade or attempted kidnapping. I admit, it's interesting watching action-packed movies like these. When the public thinks of bodyguards — men and women in suits, wearing sunglasses with earpieces tucked into their shirts, protecting an important person in Washington or New York, they think of the US Secret Service. This is fair, I think, because people know the agency and what they do. The Foreign Service is just that to most people — foreign — so DSS Agents don't come to mind. In fact, many people in federal law enforcement, or even in the State Department, don't know the small agency even exists. The Secret Service is responsible for protecting the US President around the world, but also kings and queens traveling to the United States. Let's be honest, though, kings and queens rarely visit the United States. On contrast, DSS Agents protect the US Secretary of State around the world as well as foreign dignitaries traveling to the US, such as hundreds of foreign ministers from other countries. The Diplomatic Security Service works more protective security details, with less resources and fewer agents than the Secret Service does.

Working abroad was a different job completely. Yes, we did dabble in conducting investigations overseas as well, and I have a few stories to tell you about that later. But instead of being the lead investigator, we had to rely on the host nation's police to conduct the investigation on our behalf. The main reason for being assigned to any US Embassy overseas was to manage a team providing a safe living and working environment for the rest of the Americans at the embassy. DSS Agents are known as Regional Security Officers and answer to the American Ambassador in the country they are assigned. The ambassador is the President's representative — acts on behalf of the President — and is responsible for the entire Embassy staff. In larger countries such as Russia and China, thousands of Foreign Service Officers and Foreign Service Specialists work directly or indirectly for the ambassador.

The RSO team, depending on the size of the embassy, has a large budget and staff to manage security at the embassy as well as the houses and apartments where the Foreign Service staff live. When officers relocate, they bring their families with them (unless the country is too dangerous for spouses or children) and they don't pay rent. This housing perk is part of their compensation. All officers are usually assigned to a house or apartment in the diplomatic enclave of a city; an affluent part of town that they probably couldn't afford if they were not diplomats.

Most overseas assignments for Foreign Service personnel are two or three years. This depends on the living conditions, known as *hardship*, in any given country. If you are assigned to a war zone, like I was in Iraq, that assignment is one year. But if you get lucky enough to be assigned to the US Embassy in Prague, Czech Republic, you'll get to stay there for three years, living rent free as an American diplomat. Not bad work if you can find it. Embassy Prague is a relatively small embassy with less than one hundred officers. For demonstrative purposes, let's say one-third of the embassy staff rotates in and out of the assignment each year. The logistics needed to ship-in and ship-out around thirty families each year, along with their vehicles and thousands of pounds of personal items is certainly chaotic, especially during the summer *transition* season. With more than 260 US diplomatic posts around the world, thousands of families are moving around the world each year, stopping in the US or elsewhere to see family and take vacations, going through DC for required training, and settling in at their new assignment, waiting for their shipment of cars and other items to arrive. All-the-while settling into their new assignments, trying to figure out their new job, where to get groceries, how to set up internet service, getting their kids into the international school, wondering if it's all worth the hassle.

For some people, it's more than worth it. They love the excitement of moving to a new country and living in a nice house or apartment that they may not be able to afford if they lived in the US. They love the salary and pension that come with it. They also get to use the title of *American Diplomat* and carry a diplomatic passport and the prestige that comes with that. And they love the job of promoting US Foreign Policy or being a member of the support staff who assist those who promote relations with the host nation government. DSS Agents are those who do both — promote the President's agenda and protect those that do.

DSS Agents are the primary liaison with host nation police services in almost all situations. Other federal agencies have offices in embassies, too, and I've worked with all of them in one country or another — Drug Enforcement Administration, Immigration & Customs Enforcement, FBI, CIA, and the Secret Service. US Embassies belong to and are administered by the US Department of State. Other agencies with offices at post are tenants, and pay rent for office space, administrative support, shipping and receiving, food, and entitlements such as *official* or *diplomatic* status. In the Foreign Service, the officers and specialists have varied backgrounds, education levels, and experiences. When it comes to DSS Agents specifically, though, there are a handful who never should have gotten the job.

The non-law enforcement staff, however, is a completely different story. As with any private-sector company in the United States, there are plenty of Foreign Service personnel who should never have been given the opportunity to join. Most are incredibly liberal and have a sense of entitlement about them. The Foreign Service culture is strange, to say the least. Other government agencies know this and wonder how to get along with State Department employees whenever they are posted overseas. I spent twelve years living and working overseas and have conducted investigations on hundreds of Foreign Service officers, many of whom are incredibly ostentatious and condescending toward agents. In my opinion, the US Foreign Service is the biggest collection of ignorant intelligent people in one organization. Being part of the US Foreign Service is as close to being a member of the Ringling Brothers, Barnum & Bailey Circus as you can get without wearing a costume.

A career in the State Department isn't easy, though. First, you must get the job. And, as I already established, this is terribly difficult. Once you're in, you must move from assignment to assignment, country to country, for the rest of your career. As you can imagine, and I guess many people can't really fathom this as they are just not cut out for this lifestyle, moving every so often leads to many challenges in one's personal life. Constant change and living in different parts of the world may sound like a formula for an exotic and interesting lifestyle, which it certainly is, don't take me wrong, but it comes with its own price tag. Battling with cultural differences and a language gap, the lack of steady people in your life, living out of your suitcase for extended periods at a time, and varying quality of education for your children are just a few of the roadblocks that prevent many from enjoying this career the full-term. And of course, the actual country of your assignment has a lot to do with your overall happiness.

If assigned to a war zone like Iraq or Afghanistan, then the assignment is one year with two paid vacations, or *rest and recuperation* trips paid for by US taxpayers. Two-year assignments, such as Bangladesh, can be far worse than living in a war zone, and, on top of that, you get paid less. If lucky enough to get assigned to a nice country somewhere in Europe, the length of the assignment is typically three years.

For DSS Agents, getting assigned to a country on your assignments *wish list* comes down to the needs of the agency. But let's be frank for a moment, the decision-makers in HQ will typically give deserving agents the best posts. And to be deserving, you must have a great reputation. Agents rarely have a chance to interview for the assignment of their choice. Rather, they simply submit their wish list, then receive an email informing them of their next assignment, with further details of when they will leave their current assignment, any mandatory training that needs to be taken, such as language school, and so on. Luckily for me, throughout my career I typically received one of my top choices when it was time to rotate to a different assignment.

5
Starting Over

My first assignment after completing basic training was at the Washington Field Office. For me, it was a great assignment. I was already living in Northern Virginia, so I didn't have to pack up and move once again before starting work. Agents working in WFO would spend most of their assignments either protecting foreign dignitaries traveling to Washington, DC or New York City, protecting the US Secretary of State in the national capital region or around the world, or being assigned overseas to help the RSO secure embassy operations for weeks or even months at a time. Throughout my two-year assignment, I was constantly working on the protective security detail of the US Secretary of State, General Colin Powell, in addition to working dozens of security details of foreign diplomats traveling to DC and New York City. When a foreign country accepts an invitation from the US Government to come to the US for a meeting with a high-ranking official in DC, the other country sends the United States Department of State a formal request for transportation and protection while here. The US Government responds to that request by sending a *Diplomatic Note* back to the requesting country, affirming transportation and a protective security detail will be provided while the diplomat is in the United States. The hotel expenses and all other costs are up to the foreign country.

Sometimes the foreign country would send security officials with their diplomat, and sometimes they'd only send staffers, interpreters, and schedulers. Very rarely would we allow foreign security officers into the United States with weapons to protect their VIP. DSS, on the other hand, routinely went abroad with weapons to protect the Secretary of State. That may not be fair, but that's the way it is.

The day when all of us *rookies* received our graduation certificates, badges, and credentials along with Sig Sauer pistols, I was tasked with running with the German Foreign Minister, Joshka Fischer, during his trip to the nation's capital.

"Reinshagen, I hear you can run. Congratulations, the German FM is a big runner. You'll be running with him when he arrives tomorrow," a supervisor told me as I checked my *creds* to ensure my name was spelled correctly, before putting it in my back pocket. "Reach out to Carter, the AIC, and let him know you've been selected." Josh Carter was the Agent in Charge of the German FM's security detail. I heard about him but never met the guy. "Roger that, good to go," I replied, holstering my new Sig, and feeling relieved that the nine months of training was over.

The security briefing took place later that day at 4:00 p.m. in the Office of Dignitary Protection in Rosslyn, Virginia. The AIC and Tactical Commander of the protective detail briefed the agents assigned to protect the German Foreign Minister about all the details — when his flight arrives, which hotel he is staying, which agent is assigned which position, who was assigned to watch the hotel room overnight, who was driving the armored limousine, which agent was assigned the task of *advancing* each site to ensure they were secure when the motorcade arrived; the details were endless. Twelve agents were usually assigned to a simple and routine protective detail like this. On this trip, the German FM would arrive at Dulles International on Wednesday afternoon and leave Friday morning, returning to Berlin on Friday evening. He was in town to meet with the US Deputy Secretary of Defense, Paul Wolfowitz on September 21, 2001, at the Pentagon.

"Reinshagen, you're running with the FM from the Washington Canoe Club along the Potomac River on Canal Road, as far as he wants to go. Sorry, but you'll have to wear your SPE and your Motorola." SPE meant *special protective equipment* — a gun and two extra magazines of ammunition. "No other agents will be with you so keep the motorcade updated on your location. We need to know when you're returning to the motorcade."

"How old is he?"

"Seventy-eight."

"Seventy-eight, really? I'm going to run this old man into the ground," I replied, feeling pretty good about myself. Little did I know that Joshka Fischer's nickname was *Marathon Minister*. The guy was an accomplished runner. He participated in the New York Marathon in 1999 finishing in under four hours.

The next day, upon the minister's arrival at Dulles, the detail agents picked him up and drove him to the Ritz Carlton in Georgetown in a five-car motorcade. The *limousine* wasn't a typical limo that high school seniors rent for prom night. No, the DSS limos are usually either armored Cadillac Devilles or Chevy Tahoes. Regardless of which car is used, they are always black. The German FM was agile enough to get into a big SUV, so we used a Tahoe for this detail. After the security detail checked him into the Ritz and he met with his staff, he requested afternoon coffee at Dean and DeLuca's, a posh mainstay coffee shop just off the University of Georgetown campus on M Street. Since the *Marathon Minister* decided not to go for a run today, I was assigned a counter-surveillance position at Dean and DeLuca's. Dressed in my running shorts and tank top, I left the DSS headquarters from across the Potomac in Rosslyn, Virginia, and made my way over the bridge to Georgetown. It was a short run, maybe a half mile, and I arrived on the opposite side of the street from the coffee shop to see if anyone had set up a post to watch for the arrival of the FM. As this was an unscheduled move, it was highly unlikely nefarious actors would know where FM Fischer would be at this time. There wasn't too much to get concerned with, but then again, he always went to Dean and DeLuca's when he was in town. As I stood on the street corner in my Nike running shoes, trying to fit in, watching for people who were watching for us, a call came over the radio that Fischer scratched his coffee idea and wasn't coming after all. He had a business call to Berlin to make from the hotel which would last about an hour, then he would go for a run before dinner.

"Reinshagen, get over to the Canal Trail ASAP in case the phone call is canceled," the Tactical Commander hollered over the radio. *Hurry up and wait* was the DSS mantra. Luckily, Dean and DeLuca's is only a couple blocks from the Potomac and the Washington Canoe Club, so it took me only a few minutes. I arrived at the club to see the university's row team put their skulls into the water and head upstream for a practice row. When the detail arrived with Fischer, I was already waiting for him on the trail. I was carrying my pistol and two magazines of 9-millimeter hydra-shock ammunition in a fanny pack as well as my Motorola WT in my non-shooting hand. *All right let's see what this guy can do,* I thought to myself. I didn't realize a German police officer was going to run with us. The guy was big. Six feet four, probably two hundred thirty pounds, great shape. I stood six feet, weighed a hundred seventy pounds, but I could run like a deer, so *let's get it on.*

As we left the motorcade and ran west on Canal Road, I occasionally called in our location to the TC to keep him updated. After about five miles, the Marathon Minister said something to my police counterpart in German and he turned to me and said with a heavy accent reminding me of the character *Drago* in *Rocky,* "We go back." I started getting winded after about seven miles in. Running with my gun and extra magazines certainly wasn't ideal and I started to think this running assignment with a foreign diplomat wasn't as much fun as I thought it would be. At that moment, the FM started increasing his pace. *What the hell,* I thought to myself. *Eight miles in, and the old guy is going even faster. I'm not going to make it!*

As we got closer to our starting point at the Washington Canoe Club, I saw the motorcade of black cars sitting on the bank of the Potomac and the detail agents dressed in suits. With a mile still to go, I was about to fall flat on my face. I couldn't keep up with the minister or the big German police officer, so I called ahead to the Agent in Charge of the detail.

"Carter, I'm going to peel off here and watch the flank," I said over the radio, trying to hide the fact that I simply couldn't finish the run. It didn't work.

"Looks like he's hauling ass, but I heard you were a runner! So much for that."

By the time I made it to the Canoe Club, the FM was getting into the Tahoe with his German bodyguard, who looked at me condescendingly. I could swear I heard him say under his breath in broken English, "Weak American."

And there I was, bent over, trying to catch my breath, in front of everyone on the banks of the Potomac. A newly minted agent fresh out of training with Physical Fitness honors, and I just had my ass handed to me by a seventy-eight-year-old man. An hour ago, I was ten feet tall and bulletproof. And now, I'm coughing up a lung, looking like a fool. I had a lot to learn about this job. *Slow roll.*

* * *

After a few months of working protective details — one after another — I got the hang of it. Being assigned to WFO meant I was constantly working protection details, and the residents in DC were used to seeing black motorcades zip through the city with lights on and sirens blaring as we raced from State Department HQ, the Pentagon, or Capitol Hill to the White House or one of the many monuments and shopping malls in the area, babysitting a foreign diplomat. It was exciting sitting in the back seat of the Tahoe, windows down, sunglasses on, earpiece in my ear as people watched us roll by, the tourists taking pictures of us as we came to a stop in front of some restaurant, setting up a perimeter as we got our *protectee* inside so they can eat lunch. Most of the time, people had no idea who we were protecting. Not because we didn't allow passers-by to see, but because typical Americans don't watch the news very often and have no idea what is going on outside the United States. So naturally, they aren't going to recognize a foreign diplomat, especially from a country they've never heard of.

After proving myself capable of being a dependable agent who was good at working details, I was assigned to the Saudi Arabian protective detail of Bandar bin Sultan. The Prince Bandar detail was affectionately known as the *knife and fork* detail because the agents were well fed by the Saudi government whenever protecting Prince Bandar. The Saudi government rented two mansions overlooking the Potomac — one of these huge houses was where the Saudi Ambassador lived, while the one next door was used as a guest house. A British national was the head of the prince's personal security detail which was assigned to work security and protection at both houses, ensuring only guests enter the compound through the heavy iron gates near the street. We worked well with them at the residence, but DSS Agents were the only people who protected the Prince when he was not at home.

I was assigned to the Bandar detail for ninety days. It was a great time — the assignment was easy and since we worked long days, our paychecks were great. There were only a few of us on the detail — a Tactical Commander who was in charge, a follow-car driver, and a *right rear* agent. Prince Bandar drove himself in a black, armored Mercedes Benz 500SL as opposed to having an agent chauffeur him around town. As DSS Agents assigned to protect him, we drove behind the Mercedes in a black Tahoe, following him whenever he left his house. Once we arrived to wherever he was going, the TC and the right rear agent would get out of the Tahoe and walk alongside the Prince, protecting him from harm or embarrassment of any sort. The Saudis, like every other country on earth, wouldn't want their Ambassador, who was living and working in the national capital region, to be harmed or embarrassed by anyone. It's bad optics on the world stage. Most of Bandar's movements were to restaurants; the guy liked to eat! And whenever he ate, we ate. He routinely paid for dinner for the three DSS Agents. The Prince was a nice guy and took care of his security team. It was a good gig!

On occasion, Bandar met with US Secretary of State Colin Powell at State Department headquarters on C Street in Washington, DC, and sometimes they met at the White House. On those trips to the White House, we would put Bandar in the back seat of the Tahoe and drive him instead of him driving his own car.

"Alex, Bandar is headed to the West Wing to meet Secretary Powell tomorrow morning at 10:00 a.m.," the Tactical Commander told me one morning after we had breakfast on the Saudi estate overlooking the

Potomac. "You're driving the limo." The TC was a friend of mine. Chaz Numan was his name and, like me, he was a Border Patrol Agent before joining DSS.

The next morning, Numan and I got into the Tahoe and brought the armored SUV around to the front of the Saudi mansion. With the Prince secure in the backseat, we headed down George Washington Parkway along the Potomac River into Rosslyn, then across the bridge into DC, past the Lincoln Memorial and finally, we approached the West Wing of the White House. The Secret Service had us on the visitor list and raised the vehicle barrier, allowing us to drive into the parking lot on the west side of the White House. Numan got out of the Tahoe and opened the back door for Prince Bandar. Standing by, we watched him enter the West Wing. Given the strict security protocol as well as the fact the West Wing is not very spacious once you get inside, Numan wasn't required to accompany him. Instead, Numan and I hung outside near the Tahoe, trading work stories about protective details or criminal investigations. Forty-five minutes later, Prince Bandar came out of the West Wing with Secretary of State Colin Powell. This was very strange because there was no security detail with Secretary Powell. DSS would normally have twenty-four-hour coverage on SecState around the world, so where in the hell was the Secretary's security detail now?

Powell looked over where the black Tahoe was parked and, judging by his facial expression, recognized Numan and I as DSS Agents. As the two of them walked toward Powell's PT Cruiser, parked only a few slots over from the Tahoe, the Secretary yelled at us from across the parking lot, "He's coming with me!"

Holy Shit, is this happening right now?

"Where the fuck is his Detail?" Numan asked out loud, not expecting an answer.

"Dude, you should reach out to Backstop and ask if they know where the Secretary is," I said to Numan. *Backstop* was the on-site command center near the Secretary's house. It was staffed twenty-four hours a day by uniformed police and DSS Agents. We were tasked with knowing where the Secretary is at all times, day, or night, in the US or abroad. There is no way in hell he went anywhere without fifteen DSS Agents being in proximity. Never. Except today. He was at the White House, and Numan and I were the only guys that knew this.

"Backstop, this is the Bandar Detail, do you copy?" Numan asked over the Motorola.

"Bandar Detail, copy loud and clear."

"Do you know where Trailblazer is right now?"

"Uh, yes Numan, he is at his house. Thanks for checking up on us."

"That's a negative, Backstop. Trailblazer is at the West Wing. We are here with Prince Bandar, and they just got into Trailblazer's PT Cruiser. They are headed your way, back to his residence. We'll follow them. Enroute your location."

As Numan and I watched the United States Secretary of State and the twenty-ninth Prince of Saudi Arabia get into Powell's purple PT Cruiser at the West Wing of the White House, we realized we were the only two agents in the entire United States Government who were protecting them both at that moment. How can the Secretary's Detail not know where the hell he is on a Saturday morning at 11:00 a.m.?

The PT Cruiser made its way south onto 17th Street, turned right on Constitution Avenue and across Teddy Roosevelt Bridge into Northern Virginia. Once he made it onto Washington Memorial Parkway, the Secretary stepped on the gas. Cruising at well over ninety miles an hour, I kept pace with the PT Cruiser in the armored Tahoe, exiting behind the two of them in Langley. Passing CIA Headquarters, we pulled into General Powell's driveway in the upscale neighborhood of McClean. The residence's watch officers were already waiting for the Secretary, still wondering how in the world he departed his residence without being noticed. Since our radio communication with Backstop was heard by every other State Department detail including the DSS Command Center in Rosslyn, Virginia, and State Department's Operations Center in DC, everyone knew the Secretary's Detail lost the Secretary, and Numan and I found him at the West Wing. Heads would roll over this.

***

When we weren't protecting foreign dignitaries or traveling around the world with the Secretary of State, we'd spend a lot of time keeping current with our casework. As I already explained, DSS Agents are federal agents who conduct investigations involving United States passports and American visas. Visa fraud was somewhat rare. Passport fraud is not only an easier crime to commit, but also more beneficial to the criminal. There are a few crime organizations in the world who could either manufacture or alter a US visa to make it look real. The Chinese were the best at altering visas. But let's talk about US passports for a minute.

Among the most coveted travel documents in existence is the United States passport. Not only is the passport proof of identity and of United States citizenship, but most countries allow American travelers to enter their country without a travel visa.

US passports are difficult to replicate due to the plentiful security features built-in to each. Since they are hard to make, most passport fraud investigations involve altering some of the information on a valid passport, such as the name or perhaps the photograph.

There are many reasons why someone would want to change their identity — and I'll talk about some criminal investigations I conducted throughout this book — but suffice it to say, obtaining a validly issued US passport bearing the picture of another person is easier than you think, especially in California.

If you do not already have one, it's relatively simple to obtain a valid passport. All passports are issued by the US Department of State. To initiate the process, one must submit a passport application, along with their photograph, proof of identity, and proof of US citizenship — either a validly issued United States Birth Certificate or a Naturalization Certificate. Once the passport processing center receives the application, multiple name checks are completed on the applicant as well as a facial recognition check of the person depicted in the photograph accompanying the passport application. A facial recognition check compares the photo in the application with photos on driver's licenses, in arrest records, and on other passport applications. If a record exists of another application being submitted with photographs of the same person, the passport adjudicator will ensure the names on both applications match. If two different applications exist with a photo of the same person but with different names, the adjudicator flags the newest application and forwards the case to the Diplomatic Security Service for investigation. The goal is to determine the identity of the applicant. Do you have your original birth certificate? I do. Many people do, in fact, with the date of issuance printed on it. Mine was issued in 1971. But anyone can obtain a valid, newly issued birth certificate in their own name, just so they have another copy, and it will have the date of issue printed on it. Just go to your local Office of Vital Records and apply for one. Many people have a second birth certificate; it's not unusual.

In California, though, it's a bit different. In California, anyone can obtain a valid birth certificate of anyone else. Meaning John Doe can obtain a new and validly issued birth certificate of Bob Smith and use that birth certificate to apply for a US passport in the name of Bob Smith. Voila! John Doe not only changed his identity to Bob Smith, but he stole Bob Smith's identity in the process. With his new identity, John can cause a great deal of damage to Bob's finances and personal life; John can evade arrest, travel around the world, and make his old self disappear. Why would anyone want to disappear, you ask? I have a few stories I'd like to share with you later in the book.

Remember when I said earlier all passport applications need to be submitted with a valid birth certificate? If someone wishes to obtain a passport in an identity other than their own, that person needs to obtain the birth certificate of another person and submit *that* BC with *their* passport application. If that other person already has a passport, then the second application will be flagged as potentially fraudulent because an application already exists in that identity. DSS will be asked to open a criminal investigation on the latest passport applicant, who is not likely to be the true person, or owner, of the birth certificate. The birth certificate is the key document in almost every investigation. What I have seen throughout my career is this — the person who has the *oldest* passport is usually the true identity, while the person with the recently issued passport is the fraud.

According to the United States Department of Justice Archives, United States Code reads, "*Section 1542 of Title 18 proscribes both false statements made to obtain a passport, and use of any passport so obtained. The false statement against which this section is most commonly used is the use of a false name in obtaining a passport. United States citizens attempt to obtain passports using false names in order to conceal criminal activity. A problem of proof can arise when the passport applicant has routinely used aliases and now seeks to obtain a passport in one of those aliases. See, e.g., United States v. O'Bryant, 775 F.2d 1528 (11ᵗʰ Cir.1985); United States v. Cox, 593 F.2d 46 (6ᵗʰ Cir.1979); United States v. Wasman, 641 F.2d 326 (5ᵗʰ Cir.1981); aff'd, 464 U.S. 932 (1984).*"

Confused? I'm sure you are. This is why DSS Agents attend months of training to be effective criminal investigators.

While assigned to the Washington Field Office, I was responsible for conducting passport fraud cases in Baltimore, Maryland. My colleague and I worked together and spent a lot of time conducting investigations in low-income Baltimore neighborhoods around Johns Hopkins University. T-Bone was a former Marine and a great partner when it came to maintaining the integrity of the US passport, and there were plenty of leads to follow in this city. The problem was the United States Attorney's Office in Baltimore. They very rarely accepted our cases for prosecution. Why? Because passport fraud cases weren't exciting enough for a prosecutor to spend their time on. No, the US Attorney's Office mainly accepted DOJ cases — FBI and DEA investigations involving murder, terrorism, drug smuggling, or a combination of the three. Department of State cases received little love in the state of Maryland or in the Commonwealth of Virginia.

When he and I were not assigned to the Secretary of State's protective detail, I'd pick T-Bone up in my government issued Chevy Impala in Northern Virginia, stop at a coffee shop, and make the ninety-minute drive to the target of one of many investigations based in Baltimore. The case details were the same as we'd seen in dozens of investigations — the passport office received an application which included a valid and recently issued birth certificate along with a valid Maryland driver's license, and two photographs. The photos submitted with the passport application matched the driver's license photo. The passport adjudicator flagged the application because a passport had already been issued years prior to a person claiming the same identity but using a different photo. In this case, two people claimed to have the name Shawn Franklin, and both had used the same birth certificate as proof of identity. My job was to determine who was the real Shawn Franklin, and who was the fraud — should be a relatively simple task.

As I mentioned earlier, the key document is the birth certificate. The difficulty lies in finding the imposter and proving beyond a reasonable doubt the imposter knowingly and willfully applied for the fraudulent passport. Once accomplished, I needed to sell my case to the USAO in Baltimore and get them to accept the case for prosecution. That was no easy task.

Since I had every indication to believe the second passport application was submitted by an imposter, I located and interviewed the owner of the first passport application, Shawn Franklin, who worked at MedStar Memorial Hospital near Johns Hopkins. I showed Franklin the passport application signed by the imposter and asked him if he submitted the application. No, he did not. I asked Franklin if he had his original birth certificate and, if so, could I look at it. He thought his mother had it, but she lived in LA at the time.

"It's important that I see that birth certificate. Do you think your mother can mail it to you?"

"Sure," he said. "I guess so."

I showed Franklin a copy of the photograph accompanying the bogus application and asked if the photo depicted him. No, it didn't. I asked Franklin if he knew the person in the photograph claiming to be Shawn Franklin, using his birth certificate.

"It's my sister's asshole boyfriend."

"Do you know where he lives or works?"

"Yeah, he lives in Waverly. Section 8. Don't know which apartment though. Don't know where he works. You gonna go find him? He in trouble?"

Deflecting his questions, I asked him not to contact his sister's boyfriend or talk to her about this issue. "I'll be in touch, here is my business card. Call me if you find out where he lives."

As T-Bone and I turned and got in my unmarked police car, he said, "Let's go to Waverly."

This was our first time in the Waverly neighborhood. As we drove through the low-income housing development complex, we were easily identified as the law enforcement — two very fit, white guys with short hair driving a black Chevy Impala with US Government tags, looking for a black guy in Section 8 housing.

"Five-o, five-o!" warned a ten-year-old boy playing basketball with a trash can on the street corner, letting anyone within earshot know the police were around.

"Dude, we aren't getting anything done in this neighborhood, not without an informant," T-Bone assured me.

"Well, we aren't going to get an informant, so we need to either conduct surveillance in the surveillance van at night or find out where this imposter lives."

"Or get the *true ID* to find out for us."

"Yeah, he might be able to."

I texted the true Shawn Franklin and asked him to discretely find out exactly where his sister's boyfriend lives or works. Keep it on the down-low, I told him. "Let me know when you got something."

I pushed this investigation to the back of the stove. I needed information that I didn't have and would have a hard time getting without an informant.

Over the next two months, I worked protective detail after protective detail. The Chinese, the Singaporeans, the French, the Germans again, the Brazilians. Washington, DC, New York, Atlanta, Boston, San Francisco. It never stopped, and I loved every minute of it. I was working hard, but also making a lot of money. I bought a new BMW and a few new suits. I was going on some good trips with Secretary Powell, and I wanted to look sharp. I was having a blast. With less than two years on the job, my Italian shoes were used to good news.

"Reinshagen, I need you on the car plane team to Kazakhstan," my supervisor told me in a weekly team meeting a month later at the field office. "Get with Brad at DP and he'll give you the details. I think you depart this weekend. It's a good assignment. Have fun and let me know when you get back in town. You're due to qualify on your Sig next month so we gotta get you out to the range."

A security detail assigned to protect a US Secretary of State takes up considerable resources, especially when the Secretary goes on a trip that involves multiple cities. There are four or five security teams assigned to an overseas trip — the advance team, plane team, car plane team, and jump teams. The advance team travels to each city where the Secretary is scheduled to appear and works with the American Embassy and host nation police to set up a security plan for the visit.

The plane team is a small group of four or five Special Agents who travel on the same plane as the Secretary of State, a Boeing 757. This plane carries the crew, SecState, traveling press, Air Force security personnel to guard the plane when it's overseas and not being used, and DSS plane team agents.

The jump teams consist of ten to twenty DSS Agents assigned to work protection in cities to which the Secretary travels. The agents *jump* from one city to another, arriving before the plane team arrives on the Secretary's 757, working tirelessly around the clock to ensure he or she has a full protective detail in that city.

The car plane team is an agent or two that travels on a United States Air Force C-5 cargo plane with the armored car that will be utilized by SecState at a location abroad. The enormous Lockheed Martin aircraft, once one of the largest planes in the world, is used to transport cargo and personnel for the Department of Defense. It is big and powerful enough to carry fifteen Humvees in its cargo bay to anywhere in the world.

In December 2001, I was assigned to the car plane team responsible for ensuring the US Air Force delivered the Secretary's armored Chevrolet Suburban to Astana, Kazakhstan. It was this exact Suburban which would be used in the DSS motorcade while SecState was on his official trip to the capital city. After the trip, I was responsible for getting the Suburban back to the US. My colleague, Marco Davis, was also on the car plane team, and he was responsible for delivering another armored Sub to Tashkent, Uzbekistan. Davis spoke fluent Korean and passable Japanese. He wasn't very talkative, and I was always a bit suspicious of other agents who didn't have much to say. Whenever we chatted, it seemed he was either daydreaming and lost in his own thoughts, or he silently disagreed with whatever it was that I was saying. I couldn't figure him out. Before joining DSS he was an FBI analyst in DC.

A few days later, Davis and I packed our bags and drove the black armored Suburbans to Andrews Air Force Base to link up with the USAF liaison who helped us load both vehicles into the C-5. Once the vehicles were in the cargo bay, the flight crew strapped the cars down to the floor of the plane, preventing them from shifting or moving. Since they had the pleasure of transporting us two diplomats and the armored cars to Central Asia, the Air Force was kind enough to load a pallet-based bathroom onto the plane — we'd have a toilet and running water for the long trip as opposed to peeing in a plastic bottle. *How nice of the Air Force.*

After taking off, we flew to Ramstein Air Base in Germany and spent the night in a local hotel before continuing our trip to Uzbekistan, where Davis would unload his car. We arrived at 2:00 a.m. As Davis started backing his Suburban onto the tarmac in the cold of the night, a member of the flight crew disembarked from the plane with a briefcase and met with an Uzbek official waiting in the blistering wind.

"Alex. Watch Montoya," the captain of the crew said as he pointed to the two figures meeting on the tarmac in the middle of the night.

Airman Montoya opened his briefcase and pulled out a small bundle of something I couldn't make out, handing it to the Uzbek

86

official. After nonchalantly looking at what he had just received, the Uzbek man held out his hand and the two men shook hands as the snow began to fall. Montoya motioned toward Davis, who was pulling the Suburban away from the C-5 toward the hangar a hundred yards away. Montoya had done this before.

"What was that about?" I asked Airman Montoya after he got back onto the C-5.

"Payment."

"For what?"

"For landing. I also asked him to empty the latrine."

"I didn't realize that would be a cash transaction," I said, shaking my head in astonishment.

"Sir, it's always a cash transaction in these smaller countries."

I'd seen this sort of thing in the movies but had not been a part of it until now — landing a military aircraft on a deserted runway in Central Asia in the middle of the night; unloading valuable cargo; making a cash *donation* to a guy in a fur coat and hat; then getting off the ground as if we were never there.

The flight crew closed the massive cargo door of the plane, we taxied down the runway and lifted off the ground in less than fifteen minutes. Next stop, Kazakhstan.

An hour later, we landed in Astana, a Sunni Muslim city of one million people. The flight crew breached the cargo bay door, and the chill of the air took my breath away. It was minus thirty-five degrees Fahrenheit. I pulled the collar of my jacket further up my neck to stay warm and got into the Sub. Cranking up the heat, I drove the car off the airplane and waited for the flight crew to do whatever they needed to the plane. Three of the crew members known as Ravens, would stay with the plane, guarding it over the next few days while SecState was in Astana, ensuring no one got close to the bird as it sat on the empty tarmac in the barren wasteland covered in snow. The rest of the flight crew piled into my Suburban, rubbing their hands together to get warm, and we drove to the hotel. Once we arrived, I handed the keys off to the DSS Advance Agent, who had been in town for a week by then and was responsible for lining up all aspects of the Secretary's security detail before the 757 arrived with the plane team. My job was done, for now.

Secretary Powell's visit to Astana was very brief — upon his arrival he attended one formal and one informal meeting before turning in for the night. The next day, the security detail took him to the airport where he boarded the taxpayer-funded Boeing 757. The gaggle of traveling press were already on the plane, and, within five minutes, the aircraft was off the ground, headed back to the National Capital Region. That was it! I was scheduled to depart on the Air Force aircraft at 9:00 p.m. that night with the armored Suburban, long after the sun disappeared over the tundra to the west.

I packed my bags and met the flight crew in the hotel lobby, and we headed to the airport. When we arrived, the wind chill was minus seventy-five degrees Fahrenheit on the tarmac. I had never been so cold. Winters in the Midwest had nothing on the Great Eurasian Steppe. The runway looked like a sheet of ice and the airport was surrounded by a vast, flat, void. The wind swept snow off the ground up into small tornados which disappeared in the grey sky. My lightweight fleece jacket was no match for the wind.

The cold air and wind chill caused the airplane's brake gaskets to become too brittle which resulted in a leak in the break line. Without the gaskets working properly, the pilot could get the aircraft off the ground, but wouldn't be able to land it safely. It was simply too cold outside, and we couldn't risk taking off with brake fluid leaking. We weren't going anywhere anytime soon. Standing around on the frozen tarmac, feeling the numbing cold spreading through my entire body was certainly not fun. The pilot asked the Kazakh ground crew if they had heaters available for us to use, to blast warm air under the belly of the plane to warm the rubber gaskets enough to seal the hydraulic fluid. If they had a working heater, maybe we could take off. If they didn't, the Air Force would have to fly replacement gaskets from Germany to Astana to fix the plane. It would take a few days to get the replacement parts and an additional day for the repairs. Either we were leaving tonight, or we'd be here another four or five days. I sure hoped for the former.

As we stood on the tarmac next to the bird, I pulled a Cuban cigar from my pocket. The bitter temperature caused the cigar to crumble, but I managed to keep part of it intact and pulled out a lighter.

"What are you doing?" an enormous Kazakh security officer asked in very broken English as he approached. It was commonplace for the locals to wear fur coats and fur hats, the same as you'd see in the movies, and he looked like a character in a *James Bond* movie.

"Lighting my cigar. Staying warm."

"You can't have any flammables on the tarmac."

I looked around. Aside from the C-5, a few grounds people, and the Americans, no one else was around. It was so dark I couldn't see the end of the runway. It was quiet and almost magical with big snowflakes fluttering all around.

"There's nobody else here. Just us."

"Sir, those are the rules," the big Kazakh guy insisted.

"It's my airplane," I said, motioning to the largest aircraft in the US Air Force arsenal.

"It's my airport," he countered.

Enough said. No cigar to warm me up as we nearly froze to death in Central Asia.

Just then, the grounds crew confirmed they did, indeed, have a working heater and that they'd bring it out shortly. Hoping the gaskets would seal properly, we waited silently another couple of hours while the noisy heater did its thing under the plane, no one seeming to be in the mood to talk.

Luckily for us, it worked.

"We are good to go," came from the pilot. There was a sense of relief and excitement in the air as we started loading up. I guess I wasn't the only one looking forward to being on that plane and back at the base in Germany drinking a hot chocolate. We lifted a little while later and headed for Tashkent to pick up Davis and the other Suburban — to everyone's relief, it was a short stop without any complications. We made it to Ramstein by the next evening, my mind set on a hot shower and good meal, before getting a good night's sleep. The next day, we boarded the C-5 for the flight back to Andrews Air Force Base. Mission accomplished. That was the only time in my twenty-year career I was on the car plane team. And that was the coldest weather I've ever experienced in my life! I never returned to Kazakhstan.

* * *

Upon my return to the office, I was told that I was assigned to the 2002 Winter Olympics security detail in Salt Lake City, Utah. I was going to be on the team of DSS Agents assigned to protect the Israeli Ice Skaters. You see, at the 1972 Olympics in Munich, Germany, eight Palestinian terrorists invaded Olympic Village, the residential area where athletes live, eat, and train during the Olympic games. Two members of the Israeli team were killed and another nine were taken hostage in a failed attempt to force the Israeli Government to release more than two hundred Palestinian nationals who were being detained in Israeli jails. During a failed rescue attempt, all the hostages, and five of their captors, were killed. The Israeli Olympic Committee likely didn't want a similar attack to take place thirty years later, hence a robust American security apparatus was put into place for the Salt Lake Olympics. I was one of three DSS Agents tasked with living in the Olympic Village in Salt Lake, utilizing the University of Utah campus. Our sole purpose was to protect the Israeli athletes around the clock.

A month later, I, along with dozens of other federal agents, boarded a flight from Dulles to Salt Lake to work security at the games. Everyone was armed, attracting a lot of attention from the other passengers. I heard the pilot announce over the loudspeaker that this is the most secure flight he has ever flown. *Funny guy.* The flight was smooth and upon our arrival in Salt Lake, we were briefed by one of the many Advance Agents DSS put into place two years prior, ensuring security for athletes and diplomats was in place. The US Secret Service had overall jurisdiction for this event, but we had a hundred or so agents on details which lasted a few days to a few weeks. And DSS ran the Israeli athlete detail without interference from any other agencies.

We set up a twenty-four/seven command post in one of the dorm rooms just down the hall from the athletes — a central hub for the DSS security detail assigned to the protection of the Israeli ice-skating team. We would come and go, rotating shifts, protecting the athletes when they went to practice or were competing at the Delta Center. The detail worked great together, with one agent always present at the command post. Fortunately, there were no issues like during the 1972 Olympics.

Living in the Olympic Village, I had an opportunity to see first-hand the behind-the-scenes Olympics — observe the energy and anticipation of the athletes as they practiced and geared up for their respective disciplines, noticing the different cultural traditions and commonalities. After a few weeks of seeing the Olympics from a competitor's perspective, it was time for the closing ceremony. I was asked to dress like an Olympic athlete and attend the closing ceremony at Rice-Eccles Stadium on the university's campus. I donned a jacket like the American athletes wore, wanting to blend into the crowd. Underneath, though, I was armed and had an earpiece in so I could keep in constant communication with the US Secret Service Command Center which had been established months prior and was located nearby. I walked into the closing ceremony with the rest of the world's Olympic athletes, protecting the Israeli skaters. It was a surreal moment, one that I'll never forget. I could feel the pulsating energy all around me, recognizing several athletes who had won medals.

As I mingled in the sea of athletes in the stadium, I walked up a few steps leading to a stage to get a better view of the large crowd. I heard music start playing right behind me. I knew there'd be a lot of performers there that evening, but I didn't know who exactly was performing, and what the schedule was. As I recognized the first familiar tunes of a song, the crowd erupted in loud screams and cheering. I turned around to see why, just in time to see a guy walk right by me, carrying a guitar. He gave me a brief smile as he passed by me, and I immediately recognized his face. He joined the rest of his band on the stage, waving to his audience, and started singing the first words of a song called *It's My Life*. The guitarist was Jon Francis Bongiovi Jr., the lead singer and front man for the rock band *Bon Jovi*. And once again, I found myself thinking how lucky I was to have this extraordinary career, watching one of my favorite bands up close during the closing ceremony of the Winter Olympic Games, surrounded by athletes from around the globe while spectators watched on televisions in every country in the world.

* * *

After returning to reality back at the Washington Field Office, I sifted through my case files and refreshed my memory of the Baltimore passport fraud case that I was working on months earlier — an applicant applied for a United States passport but the application was flagged by the adjudicator since a passport already existed in this identity; the true ID said he didn't apply for the second passport but he recognized the guy in the picture — his sister's boyfriend. The imposter lived somewhere in low-income housing in Waverly, Maryland, and the true ID was going to try to find the exact address or the place he worked. That's where I had left it.

Following up, I called the true ID to ask if he knew anything else at this time. He said he was not able to get his sister's boyfriend's exact address, but he did manage to find out he worked at Church's Fried Chicken next to the hospital in Waverly. It was time to find him.

Surveillance is a boring job, but oftentimes necessary to locate someone, especially when you don't want to spook them. I needed to find the imposter — the sister's boyfriend — without him being tipped off by a ten-year-old on the street corner that the police are in the neighborhood. I didn't know where the imposter lived and, although I had a good lead on where he worked, I didn't know which days of the week or shifts he worked. But the case was very solid, and I had an obligation to the taxpayers to protect the integrity of the US passport. Besides, I just got back from the Olympics, so I needed some easy workdays for a few weeks. I enjoyed the investigations, unlike a lot of DSS Agents, and I was basically on my own every day without an Agent in Charge or another supervisor breathing down my neck.

T-Bone met me at Dunkin' Donuts in South Riding, a neighborhood in Northern Virginia, and we drove to Baltimore to set up surveillance of Church's Fried Chicken next to the hospital, and we waited. This time, we didn't bring my black Chevy Impala, we brought his silver Chevy Impala. Not much of a change, I know, but that's all we had to drive, and his Impala had Virginia tags, not US Government tags. That would certainly help. Hoping that we wouldn't attract attention, we stayed in the car kitty-corner from the front entrance to Church's trying to spot our imposter. This could take a while.

After three boring days of surveillance, we finally saw a guy who we believed to be *our* guy leaving Church's at 10:00 p.m. and getting on a city bus. We followed the bus, which, after five stops in Waverly, made its way to the low-income housing project. The imposter exited the bus, walked into Building 308, but we couldn't tell which apartment he entered. We waited for an hour and, by 11:30 p.m., decided to get the hell out of Baltimore and head home. That's the way surveillance goes sometimes. Not always, but you had to be patient. We found our guy, though. We just didn't know in which apartment he lived.

The next day, I briefed my supervisor, Morelli, on the latest. "Good job, Alex. Let's identify this guy for sure, then we'll take it to the US Attorney's Office. The analysts ran Facial Recognition on your imposter, and he has a long criminal history — possession with intent to distribute cocaine, possession of marijuana, DUI, battery, failure to appear; he was arrested and spent a year in jail. The USAO *must* take this case!" Morelli and I met with the Special Agent in Charge of the Washington Field Office who gave us the green light to use the surveillance van to conduct nighttime surveillance on the imposter's apartment. The next night, Morelli and I drove the beat-up 1985 Chevy van, which was equipped with surveillance cameras and microphones, a wi-fi puck, refrigerator, and Maryland tags, to Waverly and parked in the lot next to Building 308 at 9:30 p.m. We were hoping the imposter's work shift was the same; that he'd leave Church's at 10:00 p.m. We wanted to be set up long before he got home.

The city bus arrived and dropped off the guy we were trying to get a positive identification on, but he was wearing a hoodie, and I couldn't get a good photo of his face. He walked into the apartment building, and we lost him again, but a few seconds later, an apartment window on the second floor was flooded with light and there was movement inside. We waited for another fifteen minutes or so, then saw our guy through the window. I snapped a few photos with the Canon camera and telescopic lens that I had brought along with us.

"Is that him?" Morelli asked, as we both looked at the digital photo I just captured, comparing it to the passport photo used in the passport application.

"That's him, we got him."

The next step in the investigation was to talk to the Housing and Urban Development office and get a positive identification of the person living in Building 308, apartment 201. When I met with HUD the next day, I was provided with the entire application packet for the imposter. I had his real name, date of birth, social security number, birth certificate, bank account number, cell phone number, driver's license number, and fingerprints. I had everything I needed to prove my case beyond a reasonable doubt to the US Attorney's Office in Baltimore, so I made an appointment with the Assistant United States Attorney to sell my case.

As an investigator, I had no control over whether the US Attorney's Office would accept my case for prosecution. In some jurisdictions like Southern California, an agent would meet with a federal judge and swear to the facts of an investigation, in which case the judge would likely issue a warrant for the arrest of the person being investigated. Maryland was different. As I mentioned earlier, the Attorney's Office rarely accepted State Department cases for prosecution. But this was a slam dunk conviction — something every prosecutor wanted. In fact, prosecutors typically will not accept a case for prosecution unless they know with one hundred percent certainty that they will win at trial. And this case was one of those.

"I see his prior criminal history includes battery, possession with intent, DUI, etcetera," the Assistant US Attorney stated as we started our meeting a few weeks later. "And there is no current warrant for his arrest, anywhere in the United States."

"No sir, but this is a slam dunk case. It's as solid as they get without a written confession," I replied with confidence.

"Look, Agent Reinshagen. Nice work on the case. Your evidence is clear and convincing. Your affidavit is flawless. Your report answers all the questions that my office has, and it's well written. We just don't have the bandwidth to take this case on right now."

"How do you mean? What else do you need? I'm all yours until this case goes to trial."

"Well, unfortunately, we've accepted some State Department cases in the past, but DSS Agents travel too much or work protective details too often, and we have a hard time getting work done taking State cases to court when we can't find the case agent."

"I can assure this office that I will not be assigned to another trip or another detail until court."

"Well, I trust your judgement and we certainly appreciate that, Alex, but if the true ID had weapons or drug smuggling charges in his criminal history, I would be inclined to take a closer look. But with simple possession and a couple DUIs, I must pass on this case. We can never find the case agent to pursue your cases in court. But again, nice work."

And that was that. I had a solid case, but it wasn't accepted for prosecution because not only was it not attractive enough for the prosecutor to chase, DSS Agents travel too often and are typically not reliable to be there when the US Attorney's Office needs them for trial. I felt really defeated as there was nothing more I could do. A few weeks later, I was notified about my next assignment — my first overseas — the American Embassy in Bangkok, Thailand. I never closed the case before I left and, about a year later, another agent who was assigned to the case emailed me saying I did a great job with the investigation, and it was a shame Baltimore didn't want to prosecute. He also said the imposter — the guy I tried to put in jail — had just been arrested for murder. Apparently, he robbed a liquor store and killed the owner. I'm sure the Assistant US Attorney who turned down my case was wishing he could turn back time. The business owner might be alive today if he accepted my case for prosecution. But that's the way it goes sometimes. When we can't change the outcome, it's time to forget about what could have been and move forward.

6
One Night in Bangkok

The Diplomatic Security Service created a new job series in 2002 for Special Agents assigned to a small group of American Embassies to work under the tutelage of the Regional Security Officer known as Assistant Regional Security Officer - Investigator. I was one of eighteen agents initially assigned overseas in this capacity. The position was created for two reasons. First and foremost, it was created to introduce safeguards in the issuance of the United States visa. US Foreign Service Consular Officers work at American Embassies in almost every country on earth. They are assigned to the Consular Services section to assist Americans who may be living or traveling in that country, and they are also responsible for interviewing foreigners who wish to apply for a US visa to travel to the United States. After the Consular Officer reviews the visa applicant's paperwork and after interviewing the applicant, it is that Consular Officer who decides, usually immediately after the interview, whether to issue a valid US visa to the applicant. This is an enormous responsibility as it is the Consular Officer who makes decisions which effect the number of people traveling to the United States each year.

As you can probably imagine, many non-US citizens, especially nationals from poor or under-developed countries, will do and pay just about anything to obtain a US visa, including bribery and cash payments to Consular Officers who want to make extra money outside of their government jobs. In 2015, a former US Consular Officer assigned to the American Embassy in Ho Chi Minh City, Vietnam, decided to go this route and pocketed three million dollars issuing valid US travel visas to more than five hundred Vietnamese nationals. The applicants paid between fifteen thousand and seventy thousand dollars for each US visa to be issued in their name and identity. The visas were real and legitimate but obtained fraudulently. The Consular Officer was investigated by DSS and later charged and convicted of conspiracy to commit bribery and visa fraud and conspiracy to defraud the United States. The Consular Officer attempted to launder his earnings by buying houses in China and Thailand but was caught. As part of a plea deal with the US Attorney's Office in Washington, DC, the employee was sentenced to five years in prison and was ordered to sell nine properties he purchased with his proceeds from the sale of the visas to reimburse the US Government.

The second reason this Investigator position was created extended outside the reach of the US Government. These DSS Agents were responsible for conducting investigations into criminal organizations abroad who may try to circumvent the official issuance of a US travel document by either fabricating bogus passports and visas for use by criminal elements or altering passports and visas and selling them on the streets of major cities such as Bangkok, Thailand.

Not long after my arrival in the late summer of 2002 at the American Embassy in Bangkok, a city of ten million inhabitants and millions of visitors each year, I had seen my share of American travelers who flocked to the beaches in the south, to the mountains in the north, and to the temples throughout the city. They come for the excellent food, cold beer, accessibility of drugs and prostitution, knock-off Rolex watches, and entertainment in a city where anything is possible. As the adage goes, *what happens in Thailand stays in Thailand*. Sometimes, visitors stay longer than planned and run out of spending money. If they were to ask around the tourist spots like Nana Plaza, Soi Cowboy, or Sukhumvit Road, these tourists would eventually figure out they can sell their passport for hundreds of dollars in cash to an organized criminal gang, then simply go to the American Embassy to claim it was lost and order a replacement for eighty-five dollars. Money problem? Problem solved.

Conducting investigations into why, on a regular basis, American tourists in Thailand would come to the embassy to report a lost passport, became routine. There were plenty of times when an

American would supposedly lose their passport twice, on the same trip, in the same city! Again, they'd come into the embassy to ask for *another* new passport. After a phone call from a suspicious Consular Officer, I would interview the American traveler and ask details about where they lost their passport, the circumstances surrounding the travel, where they had been, how much currency they had with them, and what they had been doing in Thailand. On one occasion while I was interviewing a younger woman named Sarah, I cut straight to the point.

"How much did you sell the passport for?"

"I told you I lost it," Sarah replied.

"Sarah, this is the second passport you've lost since you arrived in Thailand last month. You really want me to believe you lost another passport?" I continued, "The United States passport is the most coveted travel document in the world. My passport, which is a diplomatic passport, is worth five million dollars in the right hands. Maybe more. Your tourist passport? I can sell that passport for at least two grand."

"Well, if I would have known that!" Sarah replied.

"If you would have known that it was worth that much, you would have sold it for more. Am I right?" I asked her. "Look, I'm not going to jam you up over this. We see it all the time. The problem with you selling your passport is that now, a criminal gang — probably the Chinese — has your passport. They could steal your identity, which would cause you a slew of problems, but that's not why they buy American passports from American travelers who want to stay in Thailand for a few more days. They will sell your passport, which has your name and date of birth on it. They'll make a lot of money on it, yes. And they'll sell it to the highest bidder, which could be a terrorist organization. I don't want that, and I can imagine that you don't want your passport with your name on it to be used in the next attack in New York. So how much did you sell it for, and to whom?"

"I sold it for two hundred to a Thai guy on Khao San Road."

Now we were getting somewhere.

After ending the interview with Sarah, I arranged for my local contact, a Thai investigator, to ask the Royal Thai Police to assist me in an undercover operation to track down the guy on Khao San Road who bought Sarah's passport. I wanted to know who he was buying the tourist passports for, and what these passports were being used for. And I wanted to buy one if he would sell one to me. I wanted to get these passports off the streets of Thailand, or China, or wherever they were being sold and used. I wanted to know if these passports were being altered in some way, or if the passports were simply resold.

The operation involved me purporting to be an American tourist who fled the United States because the police were looking for me, and I came to Thailand. Now I needed a passport to return to the States, but I couldn't enter under my own name. I needed to change identities, and a passport with my photo and someone else's name just might work. My friends in the Royal Thai Police were eager to help.

Khao San Road is a tourist hotspot in Thailand. It is lined with neon signs, pubs, restaurants, music, and tourists from across the globe who want to see all that *Amazing Thailand* has to offer. Drugs are easy to come by. It's one of the most heavily touristed streets in southeast Asia and is very popular. In fact, the opening scene in *The Beach*, starring Leonardo DiCaprio, was filmed on Khao San Road.

I met with the Royal Thai Police to work out the details. During my undercover *buy* of a US passport being sold on the street in Thailand, the police would tail me in plain clothes as I walked along this backpacker hub. The RTP agreed to follow me from a distance and arrest the person who I would, hopefully, convince to sell me a passport. I trusted the Royal Thai Police, but still, I tucked my 9-millimeter pistol in the small of my back in case the deal went sideways, and the police didn't react fast enough. They were aware of the dangers lurking in Bangkok and agreed to let me carry my gun. I also wanted another American agent to back me up, so I enlisted the help of one of the US Secret Service Agents assigned to the embassy to tail, too. Like me, he was dressed in *tourist* clothes, and he also carried a concealed pistol.

As the police and I discussed what will happen during the undercover operation, I was trying to figure out how I can blend in with the destitute American travelers there, even though I looked like a US Marine. Flip flops, baggy cargo shorts, a Corona tee shirt, baseball hat on backwards. "One more thing," I said to the police during our planning meeting. "I need a Thai girlfriend. To blend in a little better."

"No problem, Mr. Alex," my Thai counterpart said in perfect English, "we will arrange that. See you tomorrow at the Khao San police precinct."

The next night, around 8:00 p.m., my FSN Investigator, my Secret Service buddy, and I arrived at the precinct not far from Khao San Road. As promised, the police arranged for a pretend Thai girlfriend for the operation. She looked to be about fifteen years old, but she fit the bill. A Thai girl, walking down Khao San with a *farang*, or foreigner, drinking beers, people-watching. I'd fit right in with the rest of the hooligans there enjoying good street food and smoking some weed.

"Khun Aor," I said to my Thai employee who was also my lead investigator and liaison with the Royal Thai Police, "where'd they get this girl from?"

"Khun Alex, she is the janitor at the police station," she replied. "Sorry, but she doesn't speak English. No English at all."

Outstanding.

I exited out the back of the Khao San Road District Station with my recently acquired Thai girlfriend with whom I couldn't communicate, turned the corner, and made my way to the tourist haven. She obviously knew what her role was, as she held my hand, spoke to me in Thai, and bought me a cold Corona from a street vendor. We passed another vendor who was selling deep fried grasshoppers and the sizzling Thai peppers in the burning wok sent a cloud of steam into the air and stung my eyes. The vendor asked me if I wanted one. I spoke enough Thai to understand her, and to reply, "Ok, I'll try one, it looks good." It wasn't, but the ice-cold Corona helped me splash the grasshopper down my throat quick enough that I didn't have time to think about what I had just ingested. I was there to get a job done, so that's what my focus was. I had to relax a bit, or the passport vendor would see right through my disguise.

Wandering down Khao San road, hand in hand with this *fifteen-year-old* temporary girlfriend, I remembered what Sarah told me during the interview — *next to a popular bar called Lucky Beer is another bar called Silk Bar, ask for a guy named Boon-nam there. Tell him you want to buy a passport and show him cash.* Boon-nam means Lucky Man in Thai, which I thought was amusing, and one that I could never forget. My Thai girlfriend — I never knew her name, but it didn't really matter — helped me find the Silk Bar. The Thai police were trailing me, and stopped when we entered the open-air establishment. My Secret Service Agent buddy walked past me, looking in the other direction, but came to a stop a couple vendors away to look at leather bracelets and some other nonsense for sale on a fold-up table. He spoke zero Thai, and I smiled a bit when I heard him speaking his best version of broken English to the vendor, trying to haggle the price on a bracelet. The Thai girl explained to the bartender in Silk Bar that I'm an American and I'd like to see Boon-nam about a passport. She explained that I've been traveling in Thailand for a couple weeks and she was excited because I'm taking her to Phuket for a month or so. She's never been in Southern Thailand. *Good thinking,* I thought to myself. The bartender disappeared for a minute, then came back. He told her to take me down the street to the D&D Inn, walk through the lobby, exit through the back door near the stairs, and turn left. Go down the alley and wait at Sabai Thai Massage. The Thai man didn't know that I understood him when he mentioned to my Thai girlfriend, "Forget about the foreigner and stay here with me. We will have a better time." She shook her head, saying, "You don't have blue eyes like him."

The bartender turned away from me to pour a couple of draft Chang beers for some weary travelers from Australia. It was obvious he was done with us, so I left the Silk Bar with Lek — I decided to give her a name after all, which means *small* — in my trail. We made our way down the dark alley to the D&D Inn, but not before stopping in a pool hall and throwing a game of darts and downing a jello shot.

Appearances were very important as we didn't know how connected, or the extent of this operation. We walked into the D&D Inn, then out the back door, and down the alley to the Sabai massage parlor. As we ducked passed strands of beads hanging from a beam above an open passageway, I noticed some locals getting foot massages in dirty old recliners. I couldn't imagine sitting down on any of the stained furniture in the semi-dark room filled with incense and Thai music in the background. Just inside the doorway we were met by a well-dressed but slender Thai man. He directed me in English to go through the massage parlor, out the back door, turn left, and enter the Kawin Place Guest House, then wait at the door. I followed the directions, made sure my Sig was still in the small of my back, and grabbed Lek's hand. *I sure as hell hope the police know where I am*, I thought to myself. Because if they don't, and I get searched by some Chinese mafia mobster in the Kawin Place hotel, not only would I not make this undercover buy, but I might also not make it out of there alive.

Lek and I made it to the back door of the guest house, and I knocked. Immediately, the door opened, and a Thai guy motioned for us to come in. We hurriedly stepped inside. As I looked around, searching with my eyes the few guys inside for weapons and trying to assess the mood in the room, I felt Lek grab my arm a bit tighter. *Yeah, this isn't a good situation*, I thought to myself. She agreed. I didn't know the other men in the room and assumed they were part of some Thai mafia group, the kind of people I'd heard about but have never seen. The stories that made their way around the *farangs* who had been in the city far too long usually ended with the Thai mafia kidnapping the girlfriend or wife of a westerner who had crossed them in a bad drug deal, taking her across the border into Burma, and selling her to the Burmese mafia for huge sums of money. No American women had been abducted that I know about, but several years ago, a couple Australian women disappeared. I didn't think they wanted to kidnap me, but if I led the police to this group, I'd have hell to pay for it. So yeah, I was nervous. And since Lek was also frightened, my *spidey* senses were on full alert mode.

The Thai man asked me in English, "You need a passport?" He was shorter than me, but I could tell he was the boss. He wore a real Tag Heuer watch, not a fake one. I could tell it was real from the metal bracelet that only actual Tags were made with. The fakes didn't come with the real bracelets. He was also drinking Johnny Walker Black label whiskey.

Realizing I had been holding my breath for the past minute or so, I sucked in some air. The stench in the room burned my lungs like a cigarette on my chest. I replied in English, "Yep, I need an American passport."

"Why?"

"I found some trouble in Miami and can't go back under my real name," I explained, being careful not to oversell it or appear too anxious. I stopped talking and pulled a wad of Thai Baht from my pocket. "Do you have a passport that looks like me?"

The Thai guy looked at me for a second, looked at the cash I had in my hand, then looked at Lek. He looked back at me again and said in broken English, "You look like police." He quickly turned and walked through a doorway into a dark hallway. I turned, grabbed Lek's hand,

and got out of there as fast as possible. Best not to stick around for too long and test what might happen.

I had my opportunity and lost it. The setup was excellent: I had the Royal Thai Police on my side and the Secret Service working with me, I had *buy* money, I had my informant in Sarah, the Thai girlfriend, I spoke broken Thai, was wearing my baggy shorts, and flip flops, I had it all. Except I looked too much like a cop. I guess working undercover wasn't the right fit for me. At least not in Thailand.

* * *

State Department Special Agents are many times also tasked with assisting other US government agencies who don't have the resources or foreign contacts and relationships with foreign police agencies to get their jobs done. Every department or agency has, at one time or another, asked DSS to help them with an overseas investigation or to locate a fugitive from justice. While assigned to the American Embassy in Bangkok for two years, I arrested seven Americans in Thailand who were wanted by the US Government.

DSS Headquarters contacted me in June 2002 about a *Request for Assistance* from the California Department of Corrections. Noel Phillip Rodriguez was sentenced to twenty-five years in prison after being convicted in 1973 for possession with intent to distribute cocaine and later attempted murder of an FBI Agent before fleeing the country.

Rodriguez did his time, twenty-five years in prison, and was out, serving ten years on parole. For those ten years, Rodriguez was required to report to his parole officer in downtown Detroit each month, stay out of jail, to find meaningful employment, and not leave the country. After four years of the cold weather and miserable living conditions on the west side of the city, Rodriguez made his way into Canada and purchased a one-way ticket to Thailand. When he didn't show up for his meeting with his PO, the parole officer checked the Treasury Enforcement Communication System database and discovered Noel Rodriguez had taken a flight from Ottawa to London, then directly into Bangkok the following week. Rodriguez skipped out on his parole and waived his middle finger at the city of Detroit when

105

his British Airways flight left Ottawa's Macdonald-Cartier International Airport. He fled the United States with six years of parole still to complete, which is a felony.

The US Attorney's Office in Detroit issued a warrant with extradition for his capture. Because of the extensive contacts my office had around Thailand, and because of the close cooperation and trust the embassy shared with the Royal Thai Police, my counterpart at the local precinct in Bangkok spread the word to his colleagues in southern Thailand that an American was wanted by DSS.

Americans traveling to Thailand are not required to have a Thai visa in their passport. Like all other nationalities, however, American travelers are required to complete a TM6 and submit it to Thai Immigration Officials when they land at Don Muang International Airport in Bangkok. A *TM6* is an arrival/departure card on which all visitors must list their name, passport number, and address where they will stay while visiting Thailand. Knowing this information, I asked my Thai Immigration Police contact if he could find the TM6 card Noel Rodriguez submitted to the Thai Immigration Bureau when he arrived in Thailand. This was the most obvious beginning in my search for the parolee. There was a catch, though. No one checks to ensure that the information on the TM6 is accurate. Travelers might plan on staying in Chiang Mai, a city in the mountains in the north, and list a hotel there, only to change plans and go to Pattaya along the southeast coast. Thai Immigration would never know the difference.

My counterpart in the Immigration office was successful. He sent me a photocopy of Noel Rodriguez's arrival card which listed his full name and US Passport number as well as the King's Garden Resort in Koh Samui as his place of residence during his stay in Thailand. Koh Samui, or Samui Island, is a small island in the Gulf of Thailand one and a half hours south of Bangkok. It's a stunning resort island, popular with Thai as well as Western travelers who can't afford to stay on the more expensive island of Phuket, further south. *Rodriguez couldn't be dumb enough to list his actual address in Thailand on his arrival card,* I thought to myself.

Just like the *Wanted* signs posted by the Sheriff in the old western movies, I created one for the man I was looking for and sent it to my Thai police contacts in Koh Samui, Pattaya, and Phuket — the three most likely destinations for anyone who wants to get lost or change identities.

There are hundreds of American tourists and residents who live in either of these three popular beach towns, and as far as Thais are concerned, all *farangs* look alike. But not Rodriguez. He was six feet five, two hundred sixty pounds. He'd stick out just about anywhere, and he did. A couple weeks after my *Wanted* signs were distributed to police precincts around southern Thailand, he was spotted in Koh Samui.

Noel Rodriguez arrived in Thailand on the date listed on his TM6, but he wasn't living at the King's Garden Resort. He had rented an apartment nearby, and even had a Thai girlfriend by now. He was making a lot of money as a bartender in a local drinking establishment which catered to tourists. Hell, I had been to this bar a few months earlier before this case landed in my lap. I may have even met that guy. It didn't matter now. The bar was a block from the beach and had some of the best burgers in Thailand.

He was living in an updated flat two blocks from the beach, eating well, drinking well, and had a girl half his age to cater to everything he needed and wanted. To get to this point, he had to pay his girlfriend's family for her services. This isn't unusual in Thailand; Rodriguez bought his girlfriend a new scooter, sure, but he also purchased a washer and dryer for her mother who lived in Udorn Thani on the northeastern border with Laos. Rodriguez had been living the life of luxury for the past six months. He didn't know it yet, but that was about to change.

"Alex, the Thai Tourist Police in Koh Samui located Rodriguez," my Thai investigator said to me while we were playing golf on my favorite course just outside of Bangkok one Saturday afternoon. I looked over at Khun Ad, who was walking toward me from the golf cart, holding his index finger up, using his other hand to hold his cellphone to his ear. He spoke to the person on the other end of the phone in Thai, but I couldn't quite make out what was being discussed. He lowered the phone and held his hand over the speaker.

"The police spotted Rodriquez at a cabana bar in Koh Samui."

"Are they sure it's him?"

"They're sending me a photo of him now, just a second, Alex."

Khun Ad opened an image on his Samsung phone the police in Koh Samui sent him just then. It was a photo from a Thai Police undercover agent dressed in street clothes, sitting at the cantina where Rodriguez worked. In the background serving drinks to weary travelers was Noel Rodriguez.

"Is this your guy?" he asked.

"Yes, that's him, Ad. You can even see his US Navy tattoo on his forearm. Tell them great job. Can they arrest him right now, then bring him up to Bangkok? You and I can go to the jail Monday morning to identify him."

"Let me ask, Alex."

Khun Ad spoke into the phone again, and this time I could understand what he was telling the police. Translated into English, he said, "Mr. Alex asked if you could arrest him now based on the US arrest warrant and bring him to Bangkok. I can bring Mr. Alex to the jail on Monday to identify Mr. Rodriguez."

Khun Ad waited for the reply, then said, "Yes, Alex. They will arrest him now based on your warrant and bring him to Bangkok tonight. You have forty-eight hours to identify him and claim him as someone you want to extradite to the US. At that point, you have sixty days to get Rodriguez out of Thailand or they will set him free."

"Great, Khun Ad. Have them move forward with the arrest and I'll get the US Marshals to fly to Thailand from DC to take custody of him and get him back to the US."

After he was picked up by the Thai Tourist Police in Koh Samui, Rodriguez was transported to a jail in central Bangkok. Monday morning, Khun Ad and I met him in jail, and that's where I identified him as the parolee who fled Detroit. Rodriguez stated he was surprised the State Department had a law enforcement arm known as the Diplomatic Security Service and he had no idea there was a warrant for his arrest. He admitted to fleeing the United States while on parole and had made a lot of money in his line of work, but this money was all confiscated and was on display when the Thai news asked me to take some questions for the local television station, with Noel Rodriguez sitting next to me.

Two US Marshals flew to Bangkok a couple weeks later to take custody of Rodriguez and transport him back to Michigan. It was a successful cooperative effort between the State Department and Thai Immigration Bureau which not only solidified international relations but also brought to justice a convicted criminal who fled the United States. Rodriguez was remanded back to prison for an additional ten years.

■ KOH SAMUI

American arrested for 'death plot'

Police yesterday arrested an American national suspected of attempting to murder a US official and selling cocaine.

Noel Philip Rodriguez, 52, was arrested by tourist police on Koh Samui.

Tourist Police commander Maj-General Panya Mamen told a press conference in Bangkok that the US Embassy had sought help from Thai police on August 18 last year to locate Rodriguez.

He added that Rodriguez was also charged with attempting to kill an agent of the US Federal Bureau of Investigation before fleeing to Thailand. – *The Nation.*

Philip Rodriguez

* * *

Not long after Rodriguez was escorted back to Michigan by the Marshals, I received a phone call from the DSS Honolulu Resident Office about a US passport application which was flagged by an adjudicator as potentially fraudulent. Someone had applied for a passport in the name of a child, Jason Cartwright, who had been killed in an automobile accident fifty-two years earlier at the age of three. Jason Cartwright had never been issued a US passport, so what did the adjudicator flag on the application and why did he refer the case for investigation to DSS?

The passport applicant's real name was Lawrence Meacham who, like Jason Cartwright, was born in 1970. Meacham used his own photograph on the bogus passport application and used the name and social security number of the deceased Jason Cartwright. The problem was Meacham had also been issued several passports in his own name over the years.

When the passport adjudicator ran a facial recognition check of the new passport application photo of Meacham, who was purporting to be Cartwright, there were several matches to that photo, all with the same name: Meacham. The DSS Agent assigned the case in Honolulu, Mike Maloy, contacted the Office of Vital Records in Hawaii and discovered a death certificate issued in 1973 in the name of Jason Cartwright. Based on this information, Maloy was suspicious that Lawrence Meacham was assuming the identity of Jason Cartwright by applying for a passport in the name of Cartwright.

Agent Maloy drafted an affidavit describing the crime he believed Meacham had committed and presented the case to the US Attorney's Office in Honolulu, who agreed with him. Agent Maloy then obtained a warrant for the arrest of Lawrence Meacham, also known as Cartwright.

Through the course of his investigation, Agent Maloy discovered Meacham was a pilot who worked for a non-profit organization transporting food and supplies to dependent countries in Southeast Asia and was licensed to fly heavy aircrafts, such as Boeing 747. According to shipping manifests kept on file with the Transportation Aviation Authority in Hawaii, Meacham spent a couple of months each year in Bangkok. Since I was assigned to the American Embassy in Thailand, Maloy called me for help in locating Meacham, if he was, in fact, living in Bangkok.

Once again, I had my Thai Immigration Bureau friend run checks on the existence of a TM6 for Jason Cartwright as well as Lawrence Meacham. Sure enough, several visitor arrival cards were on record with TIB for Mr. Meacham dating back over the past two years. The most recent arrival record was a few weeks ago, so there was a good possibility Meacham would still be in Bangkok. The address listed on the TM6 was always the same — Cool Winds Apartments, 29C, Sukhumvit Soi Sam in Bangkok. The red-light district. 3rd Street. The apartment building was just a few blocks from where I lived, and I knew the area well. The Thai police called Meacham's apartment, spoke with the maid, and discovered that he was, indeed, living in the apartment at the time. *This should be an easy arrest,* I thought to myself.

I contacted the Royal Thai Police in Bangkok and sent them another *Wanted* poster, only this time it had Lawrence Meacham's photo on it. The Thai police didn't want to arrest Meacham in his apartment, as this is considered rude in the Thai culture. Instead, they wanted to wait until he left his apartment and make the arrest in public. To do this, the police set up surveillance with a plain-clothed officer on Soi Sam near Cool Winds to try and spot Meacham walking into or from his apartment building.

After a week of surveillance and asking neighbors if Meacham was, in fact, living in 29C, the police got impatient and asked me to help them raid the apartment to arrest him, rude or not. I advised against this because we really didn't know whether Meacham was in Thailand, much less at home in his rental apartment. If we entered his apartment and he wasn't home, then he'd know that the police were looking for him, and he'd disappear. *We have him,* I thought. *Don't rush it.*

Unfortunately, I was overruled by the Thai police in part because they didn't want to spend any more time conducting surveillance. They wanted to make the arrest and close this case quickly. The police asked me if I could be with them at Meacham's apartment when they conducted a search warrant of 29C, and I was ready to help.

Lined up in the dimly lit hallway near the door leading into 29C, the police knocked on the door. A Thai woman dressed in a sarong with an apron tied around her waist opened the door, and the scent of Thai spices flooded the hall, making my stomach growl. I assumed the woman was Meacham's maid. There was some chatter in Thai, which I couldn't understand. Niceties and smiles were going around, and I was perplexed at the idea of this police *raid*. It looked more like we were invited over for tea. The police put their hands together and bowed their heads to the woman, a typical way in which formal greetings are made.

All five police officers entered 29C, but not before taking their shoes off and leaving them in the hall. You see, in Asian cultures, people don't wear shoes in anyone's home. Now, the police could do whatever they wanted to do, but it would still be considered rude to enter 29C and arrest Meacham with their shoes on. So, I followed suit and took my shoes off as well, lining my Nike's neatly against the wall like the police did, ensuring the laces were tucked inside and not dangling on the floor. I was a diplomat, and I sure as hell wasn't going to offend my police counterparts or the maid.

Once inside the apartment, the maid told us Meacham wasn't home. *Great, this is exactly what I didn't want to happen,* I thought to myself. The maid informed the Thai police that Meacham had been tipped off by a neighbor in 29A that the police were searching for him, so he left a few hours ago on a Thai Airways flight to Honolulu. I figured he was smart enough to be arrested in the United States as opposed to Thailand, so he was on his way back to Hawaii where he'd either be arrested upon arrival, or he'd turn himself into the police. I immediately called Maloy to relay the flight information and tell him to expect Meacham in Honolulu Airport in a few hours. Sure enough, after the Thai Airways flight landed, US Customs and Border Protection Agents arrested Meacham as he disembarked the plane in Hawaii. Maloy waited for CBP officers to bring Meacham to a small office in the arrivals hall where he'd later identify Lawrence Meacham and arrested him for Passport Fraud, a felony with a maximum sentence of five years in prison.

At his initial appearance in front the Magistrate Judge at the Prince Jonah Kuhio Kalanianaole Federal Courthouse, a godawful concrete slab building built in the 1980s and located a few blocks from the Honolulu Harbor, Lawrence Meacham got some good news from the judge presiding over his case. The judge released Meacham until his trial later that same year, and he was free to return to his job as a pilot and free to return to Thailand under one condition: he had to meet with me at the American Embassy once per month until his trial in Honolulu. The judge assigned me as Meacham's Probation Officer. As far as I know, I was the first DSS Agent ever to be assigned as a Probation Officer, and I met Meacham when he returned to Thailand a couple of weeks later as part of his probation. During our first meeting, I couldn't help asking why he applied for a passport in the name of a deceased child. He had no criminal history, made a hundred seventy thousand dollars per year as a pilot, and had a passport in his own identity.

"Why'd you apply for a passport in the name of someone who died at a young age? Are you trying to stay anonymous?" I asked him. "Trying to avoid paying alimony?"

"No, not at all. I fly into some dicey cities with supplies for the needy," he replied confidently. "If anything goes bad on any of these trips and they want to know who I am, I'd give them my bogus passport. Hell, the parent company I fly for not only encourages us pilots to carry a *throw-down* passport, but they also tell us *how* to get one."

For the next year, I met with Meacham at the American Embassy in Bangkok as his Probation Officer. Every month, Meacham called and arranged to meet with me, never missing a single appointment, until his trial date in Hawaii. He did as he was told, and I reported this to the US Attorney's Office in Honolulu. At trial, Meacham pled guilty to passport fraud. Fortunately for Meacham, the judge didn't sentence him to prison. Instead, Meacham was fined twenty-five hundred US dollars and was free to go on with his life. Although he was now a convicted felon, he returned to his Cool Winds apartment and continued working as a pilot in southeast Asia. I saw him only once after his trial, by happenstance, at a bar on Soi Cowboy in the red-light district of Bangkok. I noticed him walking into a bar with a young Thai woman and ordering a couple bottles of Chang, the local Thai beer. He gazed around the room and saw me looking at him from the other side of the bar. He raised his beer and nodded his head, as if to say, *you got me, but I'll be just fine here in Bangkok.* I had no doubts about that.

* * *

A few weeks later, the Internal Revenue Service in Hong Kong contacted me to assist with a high-profile investigation related to money laundering. An American named Jep Ginn Jr. owned a company that provided technical support for major cable television companies throughout the mid-Atlantic region and had cheated several of these companies out of over two million dollars. The IRS had been investigating Ginn's business over the past two years and obtained a warrant for his arrest in the United States, but the warrant did not include a clause for extradition from another country. This meant Ginn couldn't be touched by any US law enforcement agency while he was living in another country unless he violated a law in the other country. The problem was that, although Ginn was now living in Thailand, he hadn't broken any Thai laws, and the Thai police were not going to arrest him. They had no reason to arrest him. After all, he was a law-abiding foreigner.

To create a reason for the police to arrest Ginn and turn him over to the IRS, I worked with the State Department's Office of International Affairs to have his passport canceled. Once his passport was no longer valid, Ginn was in Thailand illegally, which gave the Thais a reason to arrest him. It was a technicality, but it worked beautifully. Ginn had no idea the US Government canceled his passport. Now, I just needed to find him.

I asked the Thai Immigration Bureau for assistance in locating Ginn and was pleased that they were able to obtain Ginn's travel habits between Thailand and Cambodia. Luckily for me — not so much for him — Ginn crossed through the Thai port of entry on the eastern border near Cambodia in October 2002 using his valid passport. The Thai Immigration Bureau notified the embassy that Ginn entered Thailand and submitted a TM6 arrival card with his current address. This was a major break in the case because we had no record of this address. It was time to go there and check into it.

Like the Meacham case, the Thai Police conducted surveillance at this new address in Pattaya, a touristy beach haven on the east coast of the Gulf of Thailand and a favorite holiday destination for Westerners seeking refuge in one of the many fabulous local restaurants in the relaxing district of Jomtien Beach. The giant Buddha of Wah Kao Phra Bat keeps watch over the city and its visitors. At night, dozens of bars and strip clubs attract an adults-only crowd like in Bangkok's red-light district.

After a few days of surveillance, the Thai Tourist Police spotted Ginn leaving his apartment a few blocks from Jomtien. From what I was told, the police followed as Ginn rode his Vespa scooter a few miles south along the coast to local fishing market set up in a parking lot next to a public beach. Here, dozens of vendors erect makeshift tents to keep the blazing sun off them and their seafood and whatever fish or crustaceans they were able to catch that very morning. The market was popular with the locals because fresher seafood couldn't be found anywhere else in Chonburi Province. As Ginn was haggling with the vendor over the price of several blue crabs jockeying for position in a homemade wicker basket, the Thai police approached him and quickly shoved him into the back of an awaiting police car. Within an hour or two, Ginn was transported to Tourist Police Headquarters in Bangkok, and positively identified by a fingerprint match.

The next morning, I met with my Thai Police counterparts at Police Headquarters before we drove two hours south to Pattaya and Ginn's apartment in Jomtien Beach. We seized evidence on behalf of the IRS including important bank records which would be used in federal court, proving Ginn had defrauded dozens of companies in the United States and embezzled over two million dollars before fleeing to Thailand.

The Thai Tourist Police also confiscated Ginn's new Isuzu pickup truck, valued at more than 4.5 million Thai Baht, as well as roughly one hundred thousand American dollars, and he was transported to Guam where he faced substantial time in prison.

What had once been a great life in Southern Thailand was now to be spent inside an eight-by-ten-foot cell for the next fifteen years.

* * *

In 2003, DSS Headquarters contacted me to help locate Howard Goose, a fugitive who had escaped from prison in November 1994 after being sentenced to a ten-year term for robbery. Goose had a long history of prior criminal convictions for theft, kidnapping, and failure to appear in court to answer for his alleged criminal activity.

For some reason that I can't explain, the prison he was sentenced to was a minimum-security facility outside of Seattle, one in which inmates spent most of their time outside the prison walls, earning money working for the Washington State Department of Transportation picking up trash along Interstate 5 or State Routes 395 leading into Canada. The inmates were bussed to the side of the highway and wore bright yellow jumpsuits as they collected trash under little supervision for hours at a time, only to be herded back onto their bus and returned to their cell at the end of the night. As for prison time, this was about as easy as it got.

The first year in prison was hard for Goose. He felt he couldn't do this any longer and walked away from his prison job, and Interstate 5 near the Canadian border, and disappeared into Vancouver. The next day, he paid cash for a flight from Canada to Cambodia and made his way to Phnom Penh where he stayed for a few weeks. He soon traveled to the Philippines and started an import/export business dealing in

116

books. The business was so successful that he stayed in the Philippines for the next seven years. He moved to Bangkok in 2002 to expand his business in the region. Since escaping from prison years ago, the US Marshals had been searching for Goose and tracked him down to an address in Bangkok based on a tip from his own mother. The IRS contacted the State Department for help in locating him, and that's when I got involved.

With Thai Police assistance, I confirmed Goose was indeed in Thailand and likely violated Thai law by staying longer than his tourist visa allowed him to stay. Upon learning of Goose's location, the Justice Department obtained an Unlawful Flight to Avoid Prosecution warrant in July 2003.

The Thai Immigration Bureau was more than willing to help me find the fugitive and committed a team of Special Enforcement Division police officers to the investigation. After contacting Thai Airways about flight manifests, we discovered Goose had purchased a plane ticket from Manila to Bangkok and would be on a 6:00 p.m. flight the next day. The Immigration Bureau set up surveillance the next afternoon to watch Goose's residence until he returned home to Bangkok.

Goose lived in a small apartment building next to Lumpini Park in the city center. Like New York City's Central Park, Lumpini was a beautiful oasis in the financial district where people would stroll around a lake stocked with sea bass, or meditate in the shade of the trees, out of the blazing Bangkok sun. It was here that the police set up a tee shirt stand across the street from Goose's apartment building, and they hired a local Thai merchant to sell tee shirts to tourists while keeping an eye on the front door of the YoolLong Apartment building, a full-service apartment where Goose allegedly lived.

When he did return home on Thanksgiving Day, Thai Immigration Police Officers were waiting for him at the entrance to the building and Goose was arrested on local charges of visa overstay. This meant he didn't have a valid Thai visa in his passport and was in Thailand illegally.

In jail, I verified Goose's identity by taking his fingerprints and submitting them in the Automated Fingerprint Identification System, an electronic database controlled by the FBI. Within seconds, the database found another set of fingerprints that were an exact match with fingerprints taken when he was arrested and booked in Washington State after robbing a convenience store. Goose was later escorted back to the United States by US Marshals and was sent back to the California Department of Corrections and served an additional eleven years at Lompoc's medium security penitentiary. I just hope he doesn't locate me some day.

* * *

The US Army contacted me a few weeks later requesting help in an investigation involving several housing fraud/forgery cases of active-duty military personnel assigned to Thailand in 2002. Allegedly, someone had filed fraudulent expense claims that reported the cost of housing to be higher than it was and then pocketed the excess money. One of the suspects, Sergeant Kean Lunda, was detained by Army officials and transported to Fort Lewis, Washington, to answer to larceny charges in the amount of two hundred thirty-six thousand dollars of government housing funds. Lunda subsequently fled for Thailand where he remained on Absent Without Leave status from the Army. Sgt. Lunda was AWOL.

After months of failing to locate Lunda, I joined the hunt and asked the Thai Immigration Bureau for assistance. As they had done with Goose and Meacham, TIB researched TM6 records in the name of Kean Lunda and discovered Lunda was living with his girlfriend near Chatuchak Weekend Market just north of Bangkok. Chatuchak was a sprawling open-air market that was the epitome of Bangkok's outdoor shopping scene, flooded with locals and expats there to buy wooden statues of Buddha, fragrant incense, fake Rolex watches and just about anything else you can imagine. The food stalls there were to die for — delicious potstickers, pad Thai, beef salad loaded with enough spices to make your eyes water, and fried grasshoppers that tasted better than they sound.

The Royal Thai Police agreed to conduct surveillance of an apartment building they thought Lunda was living in. After a few days of surveillance, the police were certain Lunda entered this building carrying a few bags of groceries.

I contacted the case agent at Camp Zama, Japan, who was part of the Army's Criminal Investigation Division, to update him on the location of Lunda, and the agent was happy to hear we located him in Thailand. He wanted to be there when the police raided Lunda's apartment and asked if he could fly to Bangkok to meet with the police and take part in the arrest. The next day, the case agent arrived with three other CID Agents, eager to get Lunda.

When the police and I approached Lunda's apartment, we knocked on the door and announced in both the Thai and English languages our presence, demanding he opens the door. "Sgt. Lunda, I'm a Special Agent with the State Department. The Thai police and I would like to speak to you. Open the door, please."

The door opened, and a Thai woman invited us inside. Respecting Thai customs, we removed our shoes, and entered the large flat. She explained to the police she works for Lunda as a housekeeper and cook, and lives in the servant's quarters located in the back of the apartment. When the police asked the woman where Lunda was, she answered he wasn't home and didn't know his whereabouts. Thai surveillance officers located outside the building were not able to explain his disappearance and were dumbfounded as to how he could have eluded them. To make matters worse, manpower shortages at Camp Zama, Japan, forced the CID Investigators to fly back to Japan the following day empty-handed.

Desperate to find Lunda, the Thai Police questioned Lunda's girlfriend later that evening at a restaurant in Chatuchak Market where she worked. She was a waitress at an American hamburger joint popular with the expats. The police pressed her for answers, threatening to have her fired from her well-paying waitress gig, and she caved. Not wanting to go to jail or lose her job, she told the police

Lunda was hiding on the roof of the apartment building under surveillance.

The police returned to the apartment building and made their way to the roof by climbing a rusted fire escape barely clinging to the side of the eight-story building and found Lunda hiding behind construction equipment.

He was taken into custody at the local police precinct, and that is where I interviewed him. Lunda told me he'd seen the police conducting surveillance of his apartment building and figured he was in a lot of trouble, so he retreated to the rooftop where he had hidden for thirty-six hours! A few days later, former Sergeant Kean Lunda was transported to Camp Zama where he was later court-martialed and imprisoned by the US Army for five years.

* * *

Later that same year, I opened an investigation based on information I received from the Bureau of Alcohol, Tobacco, and Firearms and began coordinating with the Royal Thai Police to locate a US fugitive named Richard Biggs who was wanted in the United States on weapons-related charges. A warrant for Biggs was signed earlier in the summer of 2003 in the Eastern District of Virginia. The ATF considered Biggs to be armed and dangerous. I enlisted the help of the Thai Immigration Bureau.

After a few weeks of researching arrival cards under the name *Biggs*, TIB discovered that the fugitive had entered Thailand from Laos by driving a vehicle across the border. His TM6 listed an address in Chiang Rai, Thailand, a small community of Lao people not far from Thailand's border with Laos. Unfortunately, the police were unable to locate Biggs at the address listed on the TM6. We had no idea where he might be living. Finding him would take a small miracle.

Since I played a lot of golf with the provincial governor of Krung Thep Maha Nakhon, otherwise known as Bangkok Metropolis, I asked him for a favor. Although there was a warrant for Biggs' arrest in the United States but no extradition clause in the warrant, Biggs technically had not committed any crime in Thailand, and the Royal Thai Police had no reason to arrest him. I asked the governor to convince the Thai Ministry of Foreign Affairs to issue a provisional arrest warrant for Biggs based on the non-extradition warrant in the US. Although it was highly unusual, the MFA agreed to issue a Thai arrest warrant for Biggs, even though they were not obligated. *Never underestimate an agreement that can be made on the golf course.*

Biggs evaded capture for three years by regularly changing his job and address. I was able to develop several leads — where he was living and working — but Biggs remained elusive. Learning from Biggs' former neighbors in Bangkok that he married a Thai woman and built a house in northeastern Thailand, I created more *Wanted* posters, just like I had done before, and asked the local police in Chiang Khong to keep an ear to the ground for the American, hoping someone would recognize him. Months passed, but there was no sign of him. The trail grew cold.

In June 2003, Biggs entered Thailand on a direct flight from Australia. We should have had him then, but he was not arrested upon arrival because the date of birth listed on the Thai arrest warrant was incorrect! I notified the Thai police of the error and coordinated again with the Thai Ministry of Foreign Affairs to issue a new warrant with the correct date of birth. Although we were unlucky then, we were incredibly fortunate that, at the time of his entry from Australia, Biggs listed on the TM6 arrival card an address that wasn't previously associated with him, a house on Chang Island in southeastern Thailand, far away from his house in the northern mountains. It was a new lead. Ko Chang, Thailand, sits just off the coast of the southeastern corner of the country and borders Cambodia to the east. The island encompasses white-sand beaches and coral reefs which dot the Mu Ko Chang National Park. It was a bit of paradise.

Biggs rented a home in an area of Ko Chang known for its dense jungle, waterfalls, and Bao village with its houses on stilts. It was the most remote of these houses, one which sat at the end of a footpath sixty or seventy yards from the gravel road leading to the southern end of the island. For a guy who was trying to get lost, and remained lost for quite a while, I still to this day wonder why Biggs listed this address on his TM6. If he hadn't, we never would have found him.

When the local police on Ko Chang knocked on his flimsy bamboo door, Biggs opened it and immediately knew why the police were there. The police told me he closed his eyes and shook his head slowly, knowing he was going back to jail. As it turns out, his Thai wife filled out the TM6 with his actual address. Biggs never knew about it.

I interviewed Richard Biggs at the Royal Thai Police Headquarters in Bangkok the next day and confirmed his identity through fingerprints and facial recognition. Biggs told me he had no idea there was a warrant for his arrest, but I really doubt that. I guess he became complacent over time — not watching his back, relaxing his guard, thinking he was free and clear — but that one simple slip-up with the TM6 was all it took to locate him after years of hiding in amazing Thailand.

He was taken to Los Angeles by three US Marshals to face probation violation charges in US District Court. He was convicted and sentenced to five years imprisonment in Victorville Penitentiary in the valley east of LA where he became one of 1,343 prisoners.

* * *

Alex B. Reinshagen, from the US embassy, examines documents and equipment used by three Korean suspects to produce fake credit cards shown to him at the Crime Suppression Division yesterday. — APICHIT JINAKUL

Credit card forgery gang busted

South Koreans, cards, luxury goods seized

Wassayos Ngarmkham

Police have busted the biggest credit card forgery gang in a decade, after arresting three South Korean men with hundreds of fake cards. Police believe they had a worldwide network.

Senior diplomats from the South Korean embassy turned up at the Crime Suppression Division yesterday to question Kim Tae Il, 39, Choi Seo Young, 35, and Choi Youn Yong, 31, arrested in Bangkok on Wednesday with 1,911 fake credit cards and luxury goods.

Police said Kim was wanted for fraud worth about US$3.3 million in South Korea.

Officials from commercial banks including Bangkok Bank, Bank of Asia and American Express Co also showed up to examine the fake cards, all gold, and equipments used to make the cards.

Twenty American Express travellers' cheques worth $1,000 each seized from the gang were authentic, while Visa travellers' cheques worth $500 each have yet to be examined.

Police also opened Kim's Mercedes Benz E280 seized from his condominium in Bangkok on Thursday and found luxury goods and ornaments worth more than five million baht in two suitcases.

They included pens, watches, lighters, wallets, belts, a camera, diamond and gold ornaments, perfume and seven credit cards.

Police said the Koreans bought the goods and ornaments with fake cards and planned to resell them in South Korea.

Crime Suppression Division police also searched a condominium belonging to Nattnit Achalaboo, wife of Kim, at the Nirun Residence building in Phrawes and found documents giving details of forged cards. A box containing white powder, a straw and a piece of foil was also found. Goods seized earlier included electric appliances, notebook computers, dried swallows' nests, and shark fins.

7
Walk Like an Egyptian

My two-year assignment in Thailand was busier than I expected it to be, and I learned a tremendous amount about the Foreign Service's role in promoting foreign policies overseas. I built some great experience in protecting US interests such as people, buildings, and classified information, and I was able to conduct some great passport fraud investigations, which is, as an investigator, what I really enjoyed doing. When the time came to start thinking about my next assignment, I bid on my top choices of vacant positions. Eventually, I was assigned to Cairo, Egypt, which was about the last place I wanted to go, but it beat going to headquarters. I wanted to stay overseas. Hell, no one wants to go back to headquarters after being assigned abroad, especially to a place like Thailand. I departed a few months later but knew I'd be back for a visit. I loved it there.

When I arrived in Cairo in July 2004, I was assigned to a large and bright apartment in an affluent neighborhood in the southern section of the city. My commute to the American Embassy was about ten minutes by car, depending on traffic, and my Isuzu SUV was the perfect vehicle to have for the decaying roads there. I soon learned Cairo was dirty and noisy, but bustling with life and it had its charm. The people were very different from the Thai culture and traditions that I grew to like and had gotten very accustomed to. On my first day in the office, my supervisor asked if I would manage the embassy guard force that protected our embassy. It was a huge operation — one of the largest of any guard contracts in the US Foreign Service — and I didn't know a thing about how to manage nearly four hundred people. The embassy in Cairo is one of the largest in the world, and the presence of American diplomats in the Middle East has an enormous impact on stability in the region. A lot of senior officials from the State

124

Department were assigned there, and I was still a rookie. I needed to get my footing, and fast.

A few weeks after I arrived, an Egyptian man approached the east gate at the American Embassy, a walled compound in Garden City, downtown Cairo. The embassy compound consisted of several buildings; the administrative building was a fourteen-story tower of glass and steel which was out of place in a city built with beige colored stone. Although it was in the city center, a stone wall surrounded the entire compound and measured twenty feet high. The place was a fortress.

The unknown visitor was stopped by one of the dozen or so Egyptian Police officers posted around the embassy. The man told the police that he urgently needed to talk to the American Ambassador about being refused a travel visa to the United States. He was angry that the consular officer had denied his visa application, and he wanted to pitch his case to the Ambassador himself. The police officer told the guy to get lost, and stay away from the embassy, but the man refused to leave. With his anger growing stronger, and the intensity of the situation escalating, several police officers were forced to quickly detain the man. Upon searching him, they found a seven-inch machete tucked in his waistband.

In Egypt, weapons are illegal. Anyone caught with a weapon of any kind, except for American Diplomats in the DSS, would certainly experience the wrath of Allah. The police quickly took the man to the ground and tied his hands and feet, tossed him in the back of a police truck, and took him away.

"The police did a good job with that guy," I said to Mahmoud, my local Guard Force Manager who had worked at the embassy for twenty-eight years. Two years ago, he had undergone heart surgery and had barely survived the operating room. Although I never trusted him completely, he was paid to manage the guards, and he was good at his job. He had been there long before I arrived at the assignment and would stay long after I left. Yeah, I'd describe him as a friend.

"Yeah, but they're not done with him yet," Mahmoud said in perfect English.

"I imagine he'll spend a while in jail?"

"For sure, but you have to understand — being caught with a big knife like that is really bad in Egypt," Mahmoud assured me.

"What will they do to him?"

"Oh, they'll cut his hand off," Mahmoud said casually, as if he was offering me a cup of tea.

"Are you serious?"

Yes, he was.

* * *

In October 2004, three terrorist attacks rocked popular tourist destinations in Egypt's Sinai Peninsula, an enormous wedge of land separating Asia from Africa. The most devastating one was in Taba, a beautiful resort village on the Gulf of Aqaba, located just south of Egypt's border with Israel, near Gaza. The gateway to dozens of resorts on the Red Sea coast in the Sinai, Taba is popular with Israeli tourists during Jewish holidays such as the one being celebrated on that particular weekend in October. While Egyptian and Israeli travelers basked in the sun on the sandy beaches, terrorists drove a truck into the lobby of the Hilton Hotel, detonating it and killing dozens of people and injuring scores of others. The front façade of the ten-story hotel crumbled to the ground, killing everyone in the lobby. Vehicles which were parked near the main entrance of the hotel had been tossed in the air and landed upside down seventy-five feet away. Palm trees were uprooted and found new homes in the swimming pool and the parking lot near the entrance. The hotel lobby was blackened with soot from the fire and the windows on the front of the hotel were destroyed from the blast. It looked as though a meteor came out of the sky and challenged the building for superiority, along the beautiful coastline and blue waters of the gulf.

Shortly after the Taba Hilton was hit, thirty-one miles to the south, two popular campsites were targeted and bombed. A car parked in front of a trendy restaurant exploded, killing two Israelis and a local *Bedouin*, a person that lives in and roams the desert. In the second campsite, a suicide bomber fled a campground after being scared off by a security guard, then detonated the bomb strapped around his body, killing those around him.

When the dust settled, many foreigners were among the scores of Egyptians who died in the coordinated attacks. According to the Egyptian Government, the terrorists were Palestinians who tried to enter Israel to conduct attacks in the Israeli resort town of Eilat, just across the border, but were unsuccessful in crossing the border into Israel.

Not only were plenty of Israelis in Taba at the time of the explosions, but so were a few dozen British nationals. Due to the abundance of chaos and the potential for additional attacks on westerners fleeing the area, the British Embassy in Cairo felt very strongly that the British tourists were still in a great deal of danger, stranded in Taba because their vehicles had been destroyed by the blast and collapsed hotel. They turned to the American Embassy in Cairo for help in getting them out of the Sinai and back to the city. The embassy agreed to send six British vehicles to Taba to rescue the group. They also asked for one American to be the security coordinator for their motorcade. I was sent across the Sinai to meet with the British citizens the day after the blasts and lead them on a three-hour trek out of the Sinai and back to safety in Cairo.

After arriving at the Hilton Hotel in Taba and seeing the destruction first-hand, I met with my British counterpart away from all the commotion caused by rescue crews, the Egyptian Police, firefighters and paramedics, and hotel guests frantically trying to get a cell phone signal to call their loved ones and let them know they were still alive.

"Ben, I'm Alex. I'm here to get you and your folks back to Cairo safely," I said to my British counterpart, shaking his hand.

"Good day, mate. Glad to see you!" Ben said as he shook his head in disbelief of what he and his colleagues had just been through.

Ben and I coordinated with the rest of the British expats who had been staying in the Hilton, twenty-one people in all. We agreed to give everyone an hour to pack and pay their hotel bill before meeting in the parking lot across the street. When we met an hour later, I lined six cars in a motorcade formation, led by my armored Chevy Suburban, and we slowly pulled out of the lot. Although this situation was not life threatening, the drive across the northern Sinai Peninsula and the desert was nothing to take for granted. I had packed my rifle and had plenty of ammunition to defend the motorcade, if necessary, but I was still nervous as hell. The Brits were still a bit frazzled from the explosion, and I tried to keep my emotions in check too, wondering what they had just survived. Fortunately, we didn't experience any hostile actions to the motorcade on the way back to the city.

Once we arrived in Cairo, the Brits took refuge at the British Embassy while I went back to the American Embassy to inform the RSO that everything went smoothly, and the Brits thanked the American Ambassador for sending me to Taba to help them get back home. Just another day.

* * *

A year or so into my three-year assignment in Egypt, I felt comfortable with my role and responsibilities in the Regional Security Office. I learned enough Arabic to order food at the local restaurants and carry on a basic conversation with the locals. I eventually realized that I should never shake hands with an Arab woman, even in an official capacity, because the only man that touches a Muslim woman is her husband. So yes, there was a lot to learn still about other cultures and customs.

One of the female guards at the embassy apparently didn't know this rule. I got a call from Mahmoud. He was always seemed nervous, but he attempted to mask his flaw by speaking slowly and purposefully. When I answered the phone, I could hear a bit of panic in his voice not many Americans would be able to pick up on. We'd grown to trust each other more than we planned, and I was concerned about whatever he was about to tell me.

"Alex, we have a big problem," Mahmoud told me as soon as I entered his small office in the basement of the massive embassy complex. "Aziza is pregnant."

Aziza was one of the few female guards assigned to the American Presence Post in Alexandria, Egypt, a *small* city of five million people stretching along the Mediterranean Sea in the north. I knew her because we only had a dozen or so guards posted in Alexandria.

"Great news," I said. "Why is that a problem?"

Mahmoud said somberly, "She isn't married."

"Oh, that's probably not a good thing here."

In the US or Europe, having a child out of wedlock isn't such a big issue. In fact, many women want a child but decide that getting married isn't in their best interest. Times have changed, and what was once frowned upon is now widely accepted in western cultures, childbirth without marriage being one of them. But in a Muslim country, it's a completely different situation.

"No, it's not good, I'm sad to say. And certainly not good for her parents."

"What will happen to her?" I asked Mahmoud. "How will her parents deal with it?"

"Oh, they'll kill her," he said, with a serious look on his face.

"What!? They'll kill her, seriously?"

"Yes. She brought disrepute to her family. No one will talk to her or her parents again if she raises a child out of wedlock. They can't have a grandchild who was born like this," Mahmoud said, as if the child would be born an alien from another planet. "They'll take her in the desert and kill her."

I realized Mahmoud was dead serious and it sent chills down my spine. *Was this really the way things worked here?* We are all aware of cultural differences when it comes to many areas, but I don't think we fully realize the extent of some cultural distinctions in norms, values, and beliefs — what might be customary and acceptable in one society, might be considered a sin in another, punishable by death.

I'm not sure if her parents did go through with it, but I never saw Aziza again.

* * *

Madelaine Albright was the US Secretary of State until she was replaced by Colin Powell in 2001. I had a few opportunities to work on her protective security detail after I graduated from the academy and was assigned to Washington before she left office. It wasn't until 2005 that I met her again when she traveled to Cairo. At that time, it was very rare for the State Department to agree to assign a DSS Special Agent to protect a government official who had retired. In the State Department, she was a legend and I suppose someone ranked a lot higher than me must have agreed to have an agent from the RSO Cairo office protect her during the visit to Egypt's capital.

The Egyptian Police granted Madam Albright a protective detail and agreed that I would be the Team Leader, or the Agent in Charge of the operation. Of course, during this visit, she wouldn't have the luxury of a State Department's traveling executive secretariate — a gaggle of at least twenty staff from State to support her every move as a diplomat. Instead, she arrived accompanied by just one person. The young woman assisting the former Secretary, had likely just graduated from Georgetown University, or George Washington University, majoring in International Programs, and had an IQ of at least 130. But she had little to no experience as a staffer for a US Secretary of State. The inexperience and disorganization of this assistant was an abrupt departure from the days when Ms. Albright was surrounded by an experienced and professional staff.

The day after her arrival to Egypt and her check-in at the Four Seasons hotel, Ms. Albright had planned a few hours at the Khan el-Khalili souk, a famous bazaar in the historic district of Cairo where one could shop for trinkets and incense, eat authentic Egyptian and Lebanese food, watch the dervishes dance in the streets, and negotiate the cost of silk scarves, lanterns, and clothing. The embassy provided an armored Cadillac to be used to transport the Secretary around town during her visit and it was driven by an Egyptian Police officer who had been sent to the United States the previous year for a training course on how to drive these heavy vehicles. I met the former secretary in the lobby of her hotel, and after few pleasantries, I escorted her outside where the vehicle was already waiting. Making sure she was comfortable in the back seat, I hopped in the front seat of the Caddy. A Toyota Land Cruiser full of Egyptian Police Officers dressed in suits followed us from the hotel to the city center. When we arrived at the market, I certainly didn't expect what was about to happen.

After about an hour of shopping, Ms. Albright stopped for lunch while I chatted with my Egyptian Police team. Most of the officers had already protected Secretary Albright during one of her many trips to Egypt, so they knew what type of person she was and what to expect. Most US Secretaries of State were pleasant people, easy to work with, and treated DSS personnel very well. She was certainly one of the nice ones. She and Condoleezza Rice were very friendly and seemed to appreciate what we did, as Special Agents assigned to risk our lives to protect theirs. Not all of them were friendly, however, but that's a story for another time.

After lunch, Ms. Albright continued her shopping endeavors, and I began noticing she was attracting attention from other tourists and visitors to the souk. "That's the former Vice President," I heard someone say as I walked past with Madame Albright, pointing toward her. Others would comment, "There's President Albright," or "Look, it's the previous Ambassador." She undoubtedly heard these comments and noticed a crowd starting to gather and follow her. Someone in the distance would greet her in a different language, and she'd respond in the same language. Yet still, another language could be heard, and Ms. Albright would reply in a friendly, smiling gesture, speaking in *that* language. She stopped to chat with some of the crowd as the numbers grew.

I looked at my security team and motioned for them to move a bit closer around the Secretary, ready to keep everyone at a distance should the crowd become too rambunctious. There were two times in my career when I put my hands on another person to protect the VIP, and this was one of them. She seemed to enjoy the attention and friendliness of the situation, perhaps even amused that anyone would recognize her at a market aimed at tourists. But she must have assumed that people would recognize her. She allowed a few from the crowd to take *selfies* with her. Suddenly, everyone seemed to want to get their picture taken with one of the most influential people in the world, perhaps even more so than President Bill Clinton, the man who selected Ms. Albright to be the nation's top diplomat.

As the scene was getting more and more dicey, I realized it was time to get her out of there. I instructed the driver of the Cadillac using my Motorola radio to get the car in position at the north gate of the souk and instructed the Egyptian Police to start moving the crowd out of the way so we could make it to the car. After ten minutes of back-and-forth with the crowd and plenty of photos — some of whom put their arms around the former Secretary in a friendly gesture — I let Ms. Albright know that we needed to get going, and that she should follow the police officers up the alley to the awaiting limo.

"Mr. Alex, I'm in place at the north gate," the driver notified the team over the Motorola radio.

"Great, we're two minutes away."

As we managed to walk away from the crowd, I mentioned to Ms. Albright that I was sorry we had to leave but it was just getting too dangerous for her, and I didn't want anything to happen to her.

"Alex, that's the most fun I've had since I was Secretary of State," she said smiling, as I opened the door of the Caddy.

"Well, I think I can speak on behalf of many DSS Agents when I say that we really enjoyed working on your security detail and miss you as Secretary of State."

She laughed and said, "Well, I feel naked without my DSS Agents around me all the time now that I'm no longer in Government."

I closed the car door, hopped in the front seat, and told the driver to head back to the Four Seasons. When we arrived, I walked Ms. Albright to her suite and closed her hotel room door before I turned to her young staffer, who had stayed at the hotel while Ms. Albright was at the souk.

"Can you tell me about the schedule for the rest of the day?" I asked the young woman. "I need to know what she is doing, and when, so I can inform the police and the driver."

"Dinner here in the hotel at six, then she'll change clothes and she has an event to go to tonight with a bunch of ambassadors posted here," the staffer told me.

"Ok, where is she having dinner? Which restaurant?"

"I'm not sure yet, but that's something that security doesn't need to know. I'll get her to the restaurant. You just follow us," the woman said curtly as if I didn't need to know the details.

I couldn't believe what I was hearing but decided to let it slide this one time. She really didn't have a clue. I was being treated like a useless rent-a-cop, and I wasn't amused with the young woman who had recently graduated from college.

I made sure I was in the hall near Ms. Albright's suite with plenty of time to spare when she came out of her room with the staffer just a few minutes before six o'clock. I escorted both to the elevator, still not knowing in which restaurant Ms. Albright was dining because I hadn't been notified. When the elevator reached the mezzanine level, the doors opened, and we stepped out.

"Which way?" Secretary Albright asked her staffer.

"Um. I don't know."

"Alex, do you know where we are going?" Ms. Albright asked me with a look of impatience on her face.

"Sorry, ma'am, I haven't been told where you are having dinner. Which restaurant are you going to? I'll get you there."

She gave me the name of the restaurant and, since I knew immediately where it was located, I started walking down the hall with polished marble floors, glancing over my shoulder to make sure I was being followed. Once at the restaurant, I exchanged a few words with the hostess, relieved to find out a nice table was reserved for her and gestured for her to lead the way. Scanning the surroundings, I got Ms. Albright seated in the private space away from any onlookers, and walked back to the hostess stand where the young staffer was standing awkwardly. Any intentions of playing nice long forgotten, I motioned for her to step aside with me and informed her in a firm voice how things will work from now on — specifically, that I expected her to provide me with the locations and times of all of Ms. Albright's meetings and events well in advance so me and my team could coordinate with those locations and get her to and from her functions safely and without delay. The staffer wouldn't look me in the eyes, but her earlier smug tone was replaced with acceptance when she nodded.

After dinner, I walked the Secretary back to her hotel room and closed the door behind her, remaining in the hall with two Egyptian Police officers. About an hour later, the staff aid came out of her hotel room just down the hall and used her keycard to access the Secretary's room. A few minutes later, she slipped out the door and told me Ms. Albright wanted to see me.

"What does she want to discuss?"

"No idea," she replied, shrugging her shoulders, and raising her eyebrows.

I walked into the grand presidential suite, which was huge and several times larger than my first apartment. A variety of comfortable furnishings upholstered in luxurious fabrics in earth tones were positioned in a strategic way throughout the elegant reception room, creating an inviting and sophisticated space. The view through the windows in the dining room offered a glimpse of the Great Pyramids in the distance, located seven miles away on the Giza Plateau. Jazz music played in the background.

"Madam?" I asked, hesitantly looking around the seemingly empty suite. "It's Alex."

"Oh, hi, Alex. I have a big problem," the Secretary said, stepping into the room through an open door in the far-left corner, presumably leading to the bedroom. To my big surprise, I noticed she was wearing only her undergarments, about ready to put a dress on for her high-level meeting with the *Who's Who* of Egyptian elites. I dropped my eyes in a respectful gesture and slightly angled my body away from her.

It seems, she explained to me, that while at the souk that afternoon, she purchased a brooch from the owner of an antique store. The man explained that the brooch — a lapel pin designed for women to wear on their dresses — was an antique over one thousand years old, supposedly extremely rare. Ms. Albright planned to wear it tonight but as she tried to attach it to her dress, the brooch broke. Very disappointed with her purchase, she asked me to try and get her money back for it.

"Certainly, ma'am. I'll have one of my Egyptian investigators contact the shop owner for you."

Ms. Albright thanked me and handed me the business card of the shop where she bought the brooch along with the sales receipt. I took a quick look, double checking I saw correctly, I couldn't help but ask.

"Ma'am, did you really spend three thousand dollars at the souk on this brooch?" I asked her. Yes, she did!

Stepping out of her suite, I immediately called Mahmoud, my Egyptian investigator at the American Embassy, and conveyed to him the situation with the brooch.

"Mahmoud, she told me the shop owner *assured* her that the piece of jewelry is something like a thousand years old."

"I see, Mr. Alex. I can promise you there is nothing in the souk that is a thousand years old. Those markets are for tourists, not archaeologists or private collectors. Can I ask how much she paid for it?"

"She paid three thousand dollars. I have the receipt; can you come to the Four Seasons and get it?"

"Three thousand?! Alex, there isn't a piece of jewelry in the souk worth more than maybe fifty dollars," Mahmoud replied outraged.

"I know. That's why you're going back to the thief who sold it to her. And I need you to be very convincing. Let me know how it goes."

In less than thirty minutes, I met Mahmoud outside the hotel so he could collect the receipt from me and go pay a visit to the *honorable* man that sold the fake antique to the former Secretary of State for three thousand dollars. Mahmoud was a giant of a man and confronted the Egyptian shop owner about lying to Madam Secretary about the age of the brooch and taking advantage of a good-natured old woman who trusted the vendor. Mahmoud showed the man the broken brooch which Ms. Albright purchased earlier that day. At first, the shop owner denied selling the jewelry at all, saying he never stocked anything like the brooch purchased by Ms. Albright. Mahmoud stepped a bit closer to the vendor and pushed his finger into the man's chest. "Don't lie to me or I will put your balls in a vice and slowly tighten the grip."

The vendor *suddenly* remembered that he did, indeed, sell a brooch to a kind, old woman that day, but she paid only thirty American dollars for it. Mahmoud pulled the sales receipt from his pocket, showing it to the shop owner, proving she had paid the equivalent of close to three thousand American dollars for the piece. The vendor succumbed to Mahmoud's pressure and admitted he did, in fact, sell the brooch for that amount.

"Mister, I get as much as I can from these tourists," the vendor professed as he waived a hand at the plethora of passers-by walking past his shop. "She didn't try to haggle the price," he continued, speaking Arabic, "so I took her payment."

"If you don't give her a full refund right now, I'll have the American Ambassador ensure that your shop is permanently shut down," Mahmoud lied, knowing that this would never happen.

"All right, I'll give her a refund," the vendor said nervously, "but there'll be a ten percent restocking fee."

"There will be no restocking fee. After the Ambassador shuts your shop down, me and my friends will come find you and your friends for a game of *One Hundred Lashes*."

An ancient Egyptian torture method aptly named *One Hundred Lashes* was a common penalty used on those convicted of crimes such as thievery or grave robbing. The torture of a man convicted of a crime takes place in public, so the spectacle can be viewed by family, friends, and the local villagers as a means of deterrence. The convicted criminal was whipped with a cane one hundred times and stabbed five times in the back.

"Ok, ok, ok," said the shop owner. "For you, my good friend, I will not charge a restocking fee. I will give her the full refund," the shop owner assured Mahmoud, placing his hand over his heart. And he did.

The following day, I informed Ms. Albright that Mahmoud was able to *convince* the shop owner of refunding the full amount to her credit card. She was so surprised and thankful that Mahmoud was able to get her refund, yet, at the same time, she seemed embarrassed for having believed the shop owner when he told her the brooch was a valuable antique.

"You're welcome, Ma'am. Just let me know if you plan on buying anything else *before* you give someone your credit card in Egypt. I've got your back."

* * *

Aside from exploring the astonishing sights in Egypt, such as the Great Pyramids and Sphinx on the Giza Plateau just outside of Cairo and the famous ancient city of Luxor two hours to the south, Egypt was not my favorite assignment. No, far from it, as a matter of fact. To pass the time, I became involved in a softball league for expats. The Marines who protected our embassy had a team, as well as the Brits, Aussies, Kiwis, and Canadians. Chatting with the Marines, one of them mentioned they needed another player, so I joined the team and played right field. A big Marine played next to me in right center.

Well, I got a first-hand experience of the Egyptian medical field during one of our games. A deep fly ball was hit between me and the Marine playing right center field, sailing over our heads. I didn't think he'd get to it, so I was chasing it down, but I didn't call him off. I guess the Marine didn't think I'd get to it either, so he didn't call me off. As we ran toward each other, determined to catch that softball, we didn't notice each other and collided. We hit heads running at full speed and both of us dropped to the ground. The Marine stumbled to his feet after a few seconds, but I was unconscious in the outfield, on the grass for seven minutes, or so I was told. The last thing I remember before the lights went out, I was running to my right at full speed in the outfield, stretching my left arm in the air, seeing my beige leather

Wilson baseball glove against the darkening sky, keeping an eye on the ball as it got closer and closer. Then everything went dark.

The next thing I remember, an Egyptian paramedic was kneeling over me, squeezing my hand, speaking to me in Arabic.

"Alex, do you know where you are? Do you know what day it is?" over and over until I came to.

I finally regained consciousness and opened my eyes only to find two paramedics putting a neck brace on me, the entire softball team was standing around me, happy that I was somewhat OK. I felt the itchiness of the grass and realized I was in the middle of the outfield. I turned my head to the left to try to speak to the paramedic and saw an old minivan painted red and white in the outfield, too. *What the hell?* I lost consciousness again and, from what I was told, the makeshift ambulance drove out onto the field and a team of technicians loaded me into the van and took me to the hospital.

I regained consciousness during the drive there and distinctly remember laying on a thin blanket on the sheet-metal floor of the van, with a sliding door open on one side. I could see cars passing by just a few feet from me. There were no machines beeping with my heartbeat or a soft cot to lay on. There were no medical supplies in the ambulance and no one who seemed to care whether I was alive or dead.

I spent two nights in the hospital, and, sandwiched between those nights just happened to be my birthday. After being released from the hospital, the US Medical Doctor at the American Embassy suggested that I be evacuated to the United States for follow-up care simply because medical care in Egypt is not nearly as good as care in the US. Within a few days, I was on a flight to Cincinnati.

My parents picked me up at Greater Cincinnati International and took me directly to the University of Cincinnati Hospital near the university's campus. My father called the State Department to inform my agency that I had made it back to the States and was going in for testing and, after a series of exams and CT scans, I was told by a doctor that I suffered a subdural hematoma, which is bleeding under the skin, and in this case, in my skull. If the excess blood hadn't absorbed back into my body within a week or so, I may have needed to have tiny holes drilled through my skull to let the blood escape. This sort of surgery is characterized as brain surgery.

Over the next week, I stayed at my parents' house across the border in Indiana and was monitored by a doctor every few days. I had trouble forming coherent thoughts, speaking, eating, and sleeping. Thank goodness the injury corrected itself without having had holes drilled through my skull to relieve the pressure from the blood surrounding my brain, and after a couple of months, I was cleared to return to Cairo and go back to work. This was quite a scary time, but I'd experience more as my career went along.

When I returned to work in Egypt, I did as little physical activity as possible. I no longer played softball and stopped working out. I just wanted to get out of there permanently. A year went by, and I still had another year to go before I could rotate out, but a position suddenly became available at the American Embassy in Bratislava, Slovakia. It was the Head of Security position and would be a huge promotion if I could get that assignment. I asked my supervisor if I could bid on it and leave Egypt earlier than planned. He reluctantly agreed and allowed me to bid on it, but never thought HQ would agree to me leaving Africa just to fill a vacant position in Europe. DSS didn't work that way. It was extremely rare being assigned to a great spot like Europe. I needed help in getting me the assignment, so the Deputy Chief of Mission put in a good word for me with DSS HQ. Within a week, I got the assignment and within a month, I was leaving Egypt for good to be the RSO in Bratislava, Slovakia. I'm still not sure how in the hell I got the assignment. Part of it is based on reputation, part on who you know, and a lot on luck. Time to move on.

* * *

8
Luck is Underrated

My last day in Cairo was a Monday. I flew to the Slovak Republic on Tuesday and began working on Wednesday as the head of security at the American Embassy and the only US law enforcement officer in the country. For the first time I was the boss, the head of the Regional Security Office. Sure, I still had a supervisor, but I had a chance to run my own security office. The change of scenery was just what I needed. Instead of working in a crowded and dusty city with the constant honking of horns and bad restaurants, I was in Central Europe, with cobblestone streets, great pubs spilling onto the sidewalks, beautiful women, delicious Slovak food, and tasty Czech beer. *What more could a guy ask for?* My life had certainly changed for the better.

I arrived at Post to work under a presidentially appointed American Ambassador, which can turn out very good or very bad. There are two types of ambassadors. No, I'm not talking about good ambassadors and bad, or effective ambassadors and ineffective — well, there are those too — but what I'm referring to is how they got the job they did. Ambassadors are appointed by the US President to be the voice of the President when he isn't in that country. The first type of ambassador is an ambassador who was not a *career diplomat* in the US Foreign Service. They didn't work their way up, from being a newly hired Foreign Service Officer. This type of ambassador is hand-picked, typically out of the private sector, for contributing in some way toward the political aspirations of the president, or the party he represents. This is known as a *political appointee.*

Many times, politically appointed ambassadors are friends or colleagues of the president who appoints them. Maybe they were in business together at some point, or the appointee donated a truckload of cash to help get the president elected. But make no mistake about it, a political appointee is offered the job as a reward for being a political friend of the current president. Once someone earns, or is given, the title of Ambassador, then that title stays with that person for the rest of their lives.

Skip Vallee, our Ambassador, and my boss at the American Embassy in Slovakia, was the owner of *R.L. Vallee, Inc.*, a Vermont-based energy company, owner of the *Maplefields* convenience store chain, and an owner of a fuel distribution company, among several other executive level positions. Vallee was appointed by President Bush to the Advisory Committee for Trade Policy and Negotiation and later served as a member of the Republican National Convention. He was also appointed by President Bush to serve as a Political Appointee Ambassador to the Slovak Republic and did so from August 2005 to December 2007.

President Bush was in office eight years, from 2001 to 2009. His time as President of the United States was drawing to a close and *43* wanted to reward yet another buddy of his and give him the title of Ambassador, so that's what he did. Vincent Obsitnik was appointed by President Bush to various presidential delegations leading up to become the Ambassador to the Slovak Republic in 2007, taking over the reins for Ambassador Vallee, who I was sorry to see replaced by the same president who had appointed him. Mr. Vallee had his spot in the limelight for sixteen months while Mr. Obsitnik carried the torch for thirteen months. This isn't to say that neither deserved the role nor were not qualified. Skip obtained his MBA from the Wharton School at Penn in Biology, while Vincent graduated from the US Naval Academy and received his MBA from American University.

Both were great ambassadors. They both served for a limited time, as a reward by the president, and can now claim the title of *Former Ambassador* for the rest of their lives. Not bad work, if you can find it.

The other type of ambassador is a *career ambassador*. As with political appointees, career ambassadors are nominated by the sitting US President to represent him at an American Embassy in a country with diplomatic ties to the United States. Career ambassadors have made the Foreign Service their career and worked their way up the food chain. Being an American Ambassador is the pinnacle of a US Foreign Service career for those who aspire to be the top diplomat assigned to a foreign country. But just because it is an incredibly difficult title to achieve, not all ambassadors do a great job. Although the title and responsibilities are incredibly lofty, and only a few lucky ones reach the level of ambassador, not all are deserving. Some of them, it seems, have just put their time in the Foreign Service and are willing to live in a difficult place. We all must, at some point, if we wanted to keep getting promoted or get assigned to a nice place once or twice in our career. Well, Bratislava is one of those places.

Everyone asks me, at some point, which assignment was my favorite. Well, I loved Thailand, but that wasn't my favorite post. Slovakia was far and away my favorite. Not because it's Central Europe or it's a beautiful country with friendly people and delicious food, and not because I had a terrific job and worked for great ambassadors. I met my dream girl there. Daniela was a local Slovak woman and the prettiest in the country. After a few work encounters — Daniela was the Marketing Manager for the American Chamber of Commerce in Slovakia which cooperated with the embassy on a regular basis — I built up enough courage to ask her out for drinks and, to my surprise, she agreed. We have been soulmates ever since. We were married the following year, and she left everything — her family and friends, her career, and her country — to move around the world with me, living our Foreign Service lifestyle.

Attending cocktail parties with diplomats from other countries was a great way to develop strong ties and build friendships with our allies. When the American Ambassador asked me to go on a fishing trip with the other ambassadors assigned to Bratislava, I agreed and thought we would go together. Instead, I went in his place. This was the first and only time in my career that I was the Acting US Ambassador, representing American interests in the Slovak Republic on behalf of the US Government.

Well, this sounds exciting, but the *fishing trip* was anything but *fishing*. Instead, it was a group dinner on a farm, in a barn, with plenty of alcohol. I soon found myself downing shots of *slivovica* with the Russian Ambassador to Slovakia as well as the Slovak Interior Minister. *Slivovica* is a double-distilled Slovak liquor using traditional five-hundred-year-old methods resulting in a one-hundred proof spirit.

"Are we going fishing after dinner?" I asked the minister in the Slovak language.

"Yes, there is a fishpond outside. Go out there and tell the guy with the net which fish you'd like him to catch for you."

As a good sport, I exited the barn with my third shot of liquor in hand in search of the fishpond. Well, there was no fishpond, but there was a large, plastic container with water and a bunch of fish in it! I pointed to a big carp and told the guy with a net to snag it for me. He did, along with a large catfish, for good measure I guessed. So, I took it home with me in a plastic bag, still alive. Poor Daniela, my soon-to-be-wife, came home from work just after I got there and discovered a black plastic bag thrashing around on the front porch. Upon taking a few moments to share the details about our days, and particularly my *fishing expedition*, it became obvious it would be her job to deal with the fish. Tired after a full day at the office, she went to change her clothes before she started with the task at hand. Due to the lack of a better instrument, she had to whack the damned fish with a frying pan a few times to kill it, then she proceeded to cut the head off and gut it. I swear the fish was still moving as I watched her every move with the big knife over her shoulder. To my amazement, she didn't hesitate for a second handling the slippery creatures, and I knew I was about to marry good. Now I know why the Ambassador asked me to go in his place! After three years in Slovakia — which was an absolute gem of a country in Central Europe — I was assigned to San Diego for two years before we packed our lives once again and moved to South Central Asia.

9
What Have I Gotten Myself Into?

On the way to my next assignment, I stopped in DSS HQ for a few days of consultations with the Regional Director for the South-Central Asian office of International Programs. My parents made the drive from Cincinnati to meet with my wife and I and our two young children in Rosslyn, Virginia, before we left the country for the next two years, and maybe longer. After their long drive from Ohio, they settled into a Residence Inn just down the street from our hotel and we met them for dinner in DC. Although I had a few meetings the next morning, I'd be finished by noon and we planned on going to the Newseum museum on Constitution Avenue, a museum DSS would take foreign dignitaries to during protective security operations.

"Dad, I have some meetings in the morning, but if you'd like a better cup of coffee in the morning instead of the hotel coffee, there's a Starbucks on Lynn Street," I mentioned to my father, doubting he'd pay five dollars for a cup of coffee.

The next morning after my meetings at HQ to discuss the work I'd be doing and challenges I'd face living and working in Bangladesh, I asked my father if he found Starbucks Coffee next to my headquarters building. He did.

"You probably saw a bunch of DSS Agents there, since it's the nearest coffee shop to my headquarters building."

"Well, I saw a bunch of younger looking guys dressed in suits. I'm not sure if they were agents, but everyone seemed full of themselves."

In just a few words, my father summed up my agency.

"Yeah, that's the epitome of being a DSS Agent, unfortunately. Everyone nowadays seems full of themselves. Entitled. They *are* special agents, carry a black passport and badge, travel the world, make a lot of money, and feel that they're irreplaceable. But they're certainly *not.* I

144

know there are a thousand people that could replace me, but the younger agents don't see it that way. It wasn't like that when I started ten years ago."

A few days later, we said goodbye to my parents and boarded our flight to Dubai, then onward to Bangladesh.

We arrived at Dhaka International Airport during an August sweltering heatwave. The trip took us twenty-two hours, and we were completely exhausted and fed up with airports. Traveling with small children is never easy, but to move completely across the globe is certainly no small task. To make matters worse, it took another three hours for our luggage to arrive at baggage claim. Our first impressions at this point were less than favorable, accentuated even more by the fact we were all tired and needed a good shower, and perhaps some decent food. The incompetence of the baggage handlers at the airport and the *laissez-faire* attitude of the Bangladesh people got me wondering if I had made a mistake bidding on this assignment. No matter how prepared we were, or the amount of (low) expectations, one can never fully understand the extent of the poverty and cultural differences unless they visit a place like this. Let me just say it was quite a shock to get off that plane and step into the open-air terminal — hot and humid air filled with the pungent odor of exhausted travelers and airport workers who, it seemed, had not bathed in days. Hundreds of flies and mosquitos were encompassing us in every direction, with no escape, as our clothes stuck to our sweaty, exhausted bodies. Yes, in that moment, I had a lot of doubts in my mind about taking on this assignment.

After what seemed like a never-ending wait for our bags while battling off the *curious* locals, we found the embassy driver waiting for us outside with an embassy motor pool van and bottled water and loaded the vehicle. Finally, we set off toward our assigned housing, paid for by American taxpayers, where we would live for the next two years. On the drive to the diplomatic enclave where our house was located, we passed through several awful neighborhoods loaded with crumbling buildings, gravel roads, trash lining the streets, and dirt everywhere. Dhaka, Bangladesh, was consistently among the least livable cities in the world when we arrived, so why am I going there with my wife and two kids? The State Department considered this posting a thirty-five percent hardship post, one of the worst in the world. Did I mention the crowds? The population in Bangladesh is one hundred sixty million people. Imagine roughly half the population of the United States living in an area the size of the state of Georgia.

With so many people living in such a small country, the Bangladesh government was unable to supply power for the people living there and, as such, instituted rolling blackouts. This type of blackout doesn't exist in the United States. In fact, we can turn the lights on at home, and they will not go out unless you don't pay the energy bill. It's not that way in Dhaka. The government shuts down power to part of the city eleven times each day, blacking it out, leaving it with no power for thirty minutes or so. Since this sort of lifestyle isn't reasonable for an American diplomat assigned to Bangladesh, the embassy provides generators at all the residences in the embassy housing pool. The generator for my house was the size of a pickup truck and was on a slab of concrete in the front yard with a metal roof over it. When it came on throughout the day and night, it was so loud it rattled the windows. We were unable to sleep through the night for two years. We were either awakened by the sound of the generator or by the smell of the diesel fuel which filled the house, or both.

The bugs were so bad inside the house, we had an outdoor bug zapper in our living room. Even with the windows closed and the air conditioners running every day, the mosquitos got into the house. Hell, we even had to sleep with bug netting over and around our beds to keep from getting bitten alive each night. Some folks in the embassy came down with dengue fever. Dust and smoke from the city emanated through cracks in the walls and gaps around the windows which blackened the tile floors, the kitchen counters, and our kids' toys. Our housekeeper would clean the house every day, just to start all over again the next day. The tap water was so contaminated, we not only washed dishes with distilled water, but we had to put bleach in the distilled water to kill all the bacteria, and then rinse the dishes with the distilled water again. Vegetables sold at the local markets in the diplomatic enclave were sometimes grown by using human feces as fertilizer. It was so bad there, I contracted food poisoning three times during my tour by eating food at the American Embassy cafeteria, which is supposed to be safe! That was the sickest I've ever been in my entire life.

What have I gotten us into?

When we first arrived at our house, which had a brick wall around it for security reasons, a small guard booth was located on the inside corner of the lot near the old metal gate, but no guard was there. The motor pool driver got out to open the gate leading from the street to the carport connected to the side of the house and the main door. Our housing assignment was quite good considering the circumstances, but I still didn't know what to expect in terms of living conditions there. I knew it was bad, but I had no idea just how difficult it would be to live there for the next two years.

When American diplomats arrive at their assigned post, they are usually given one day off work to adjust to the time difference as well as to sort out personal matters. Bangladesh was twelve hours ahead of DC, so one day to acclimate wasn't nearly enough. And there is not much time rest on that first day as most in the Foreign Service utilize it to shop for groceries, unpack and get situated in their new residence and get local SIM cards for cell phones, which was exactly what we did. My wife and I were astonished at the poverty and dirty streets, the homelessness, and the sight of a grimy local guy peeing on the sidewalk due to the lack of public restrooms. This assignment was definitely going to be a *slow roll.*

On the second morning in country, a colleague from the embassy would arrange for transportation for you to get to the embassy. Fortunately for me, our house was only a few blocks away. The American Embassy in Dhaka is set on seven acres of land near the diplomatic residences — prime real estate. It looked like an old prison that was vacant and no longer in use. From a security standpoint, I loved it. But I was in the minority. Most Foreign Service personnel don't care about security at all. They want to work in a new office building and have the freedom to go to a Starbucks. When you bid on a thirty-five percent hardship post, you must assume the worst living conditions in the US Foreign Service. The nearest Starbucks was a two-hour flight to the east, in Bangkok.

Being posted to Bangladesh was a great assignment, aside from the difficult circumstances and living conditions. The expats stuck together, and there were plenty of foreign diplomatic missions in Bangladesh. My wife got a great job with a Top Secret security clearance at the British High Commission, which is the same as an American Embassy, so we hung out with the Brits quite often. We met and spent a lot of time with expats from Canada, Norway, and Finland, too. The Germans brought in authentic beer and cuisine to hold a fantastic Oktoberfest celebration at the German Embassy, where I downed shots of vodka with my Russian and Israeli counterparts. Our social schedule was packed with things to do. The tour in Dhaka turned out to be one of the best assignments we had. But it wasn't all fun and games.

As an expat, it was very common to have a local personal driver, as well as a cook and housekeeper. The household staff services were dirt cheap for western standards, which certainly helped as they were a real necessity in this part of the world. *Ayi,* or a housekeeper, would not only clean and help with children, but she was a valuable asset when it came to shopping for produce and other items which we were not able to purchase at the American commissary. A trip to one of the local markets was a true *experience*, to say the least. A personal driver was arguably even more essential to one's day-to-day life in Dhaka. The traffic in this country followed no rules or reason, there were no traffic signs and, worst of all, no traffic lights. Imagine that! The intersections and traffic circles were commanded by cars' honking — the loudest, most insistent, and pushy driver had the right of way. It was a true skill to drive and survive on these roads.

One Saturday afternoon, several months after we arrived, my wife was coming back from running some errands in the Gulshan district of the diplomatic enclave. This was before we hired a driver, so she was driving our Mercedes SUV herself. When a car with local tags abruptly stopped in front of her for no reason, she was unable to stop in time. She tapped the rear bumper of that car — this is very common and goes with the driving habits here, and most people don't stop to check out the damage; they just keep driving. All the cars are dented in Dhaka. A street might be wide enough for two lanes of traffic, but four rows of vehicles line up, trying to get to where they need to go, inch by inch, a cacophony of horns muffling the drivers' yelling and cursing through their open windows. In this case though, the group of young Bangladeshis in the Toyota sedan in front of her had different plans.

Mercedes Benz vehicles with diplomatic tags were certainly a target, and these guys wanted it. We were briefed about different scenarios that might potentially arise; the road rage directed toward expats, and how to handle them as soon as we first arrived in the country. But it's one thing to sit through a security briefing, and a completely different thing to experience something like that. The car in front of her waited for a few seconds, then started driving again, turning right onto the main road, heading in the same direction as her signaling light suggested. They let her drive past, looked inside and saw a beautiful woman by herself driving it, and suddenly started honking at her and tailing her very closely. She wasn't having any of that and knew how to drive defensively. She sped up and continued to make her way through traffic that was, luckily, moving along well. Out of nowhere, one car turned into two and she became aware they were trying to get around her and corner her. The Toyota sped up again, managed to pull in front of her, with the other car coming up on her left, blocking her path as she came to a stop. The local gang members got out of both vehicles and walked toward our SUV, yelling at her that she needs to pay cash for the damage she caused when she bumped into their car. The minor accident was completely staged, of course, and they thought they could intimidate her. She is petite but knows how to handle herself. The gang members kept yelling at her to get out of the car and when she refused, they tried to open the doors, hitting, and kicking the car in the process, but didn't win the struggle. One of the men broke the sideview mirror off the driver's door and continued shouting at her to open the door, a baseball bat in his hands. Who knows what they were capable of? Not to mention the rest of the traffic flowed uninterrupted, none of the locals caring to stop and intervene. Remembering her driver training in these situations, while keeping her eye on the passing traffic looking for an opening, she tapped the gas to make the car lurch forward, making them jump out of the way. She then quickly put the SUV in reverse, backing up a few feet, and maneuvering the car around, leaving those guys in her rear-view mirror. She raced down the street, noticing they ensued to follow her again and, instead of going home, she drove straight to the American Embassy for safety. Seeing the guard lifting the vehicle barrier to allow her past the first checkpoint, they decided not to mess with the feisty brunette driving the tank of an SUV. Welcome to Bangladesh.

Bangladesh is known for producing textiles and dishes, which are shipped all over the world. If you look at the clothes in your closet, it is a guarantee some of those shirts or jeans, or the sheets on your bed, were made in one of the many factories outside of Dhaka. Because of this, and because western countries don't want ISIS to set up shop in Bangladesh, a ton of foreign aid flowed into the country. Between the United States, Great Britain, and Australia, half a billion dollars of assistance per year made its way into the coffers of those who ran the country. It was a true example of the *haves* and the *have nots.*

* * *

A bit more than one year into my assignment, I was at home on a weekend when a Bangladeshi who I didn't know knocked on the gate. Our security guard named Ali apparently knew this man and opened the gate to let him into our front yard. They talked for a minute or two on the front lawn before Ali turned to me and spoke in his best broken English, managing to translate their conversation.

"Mr. Alex," Ali said, "this is a friend, he works at Mr. Gary's house as gardener. His name Ahmed. He say Mr. Gary hit on him today in the yard."

"Hit on him? What does he mean by that, Ali? Can he be more specific?"

"Yes. He say Mr. Gary tell him clean dog poop in yard but Ahmed say, No. And then Mr. Gary hit Ahmed with ... like this," Ali said as he demonstrated exactly how Gary hit Ahmed with a closed fist, but he didn't know how to say fist in English.

Dogs are a problem in Bangladesh, and many people don't like dogs because they carry diseases like rabies — dog bites are extremely common there, especially among children. I wondered if Ahmed had a son or nephew who had been bitten by one of the hundred thousand stray dogs in the city.

"Ali, ask Ahmed if one of his jobs is to clean the dog poop up in Mr. Gary's yard."

Ali asked, and the reply was, "No, he never agree to that. He hate dogs, Mr. Alex."

"Ok, ask him if I could take a picture or two of the wounds on his face."

"He say you can."

I took half a dozen photos of Ahmed's face which showed the visible injuries caused by my colleague, Gary, from hitting Ahmed five times. I made a few notes on a notepad to include Ahmed's last name, when he started working for Gary, and his responsibilities as a gardener — basic information I'd need for my report.

I knew Gary well. He worked in IT at the American Embassy and arrived a month after I did. He didn't seem to be a violent guy, so it surprised me that he beat the hell out of Ahmed, who, like most Bangladeshi males, was about five feet five and weighed maybe a hundred twenty pounds. Gary was five eleven, one ninety.

American diplomats need to behave themselves. If they don't, they can be removed from Post by the Ambassador. Occasionally, the Regional Security Office conducts investigations against colleagues; American employees at the embassy. People do stupid stuff, and this was one of those times.

Although I didn't have to, I called my supervisor, Dan, who was on a personal trip to Phnom Penh, Cambodia. He was out of the country which meant, as the Deputy RSO, I oversaw all security matters in Bangladesh until he returned. He had been in DSS for a long time and couldn't seem to get promoted as quickly as he thought he deserved to be. But I knew better. He just wasn't going to get promoted again no matter how good a job he did as head of security in Bangladesh. For one, he wasn't terribly bright. I liked him, though, as a person, but not as a supervisor.

"Dan, sorry to call you on a Saturday. Do you have a minute?" I asked.

"Sure, what's up?"

"Gary allegedly punched his gardener out today. The gardener knew where I lived, so he came down to my house to tell me about it. He has physical manifestations of injury on his face, Dan. It's not good."

"Why did Gary hit him?" he asked.

"Apparently, Gary asked his gardener to clean up the dog shit in the front yard. Ahmed told Gary that isn't in his job description, or something to that affect. Ahmed hates dogs."

"Did you talk to Gary about it?"

"No, you're the first person I called."

"Ok, so what's your plan?"

"Dan, I need to call the DCM to let him know, and I'll call the duty agent in OPR back in Washington. It's 2:15 a.m. there, but we better ensure this assault is reported right away. I don't think Ahmed will go to the Bangladeshi PD over this, but if he does and we haven't done anything about it, it's going to look very bad on you as well as on me."

"Alex, I don't think it's a good idea to inform headquarters of this. I have a meeting with the DCM on Tuesday morning. I'll bring it up then. Gotta go, my wife wants to buy another frigging set of dishes so I have to talk her off the ledge." Click.

The chain of command at the embassy, from the top down, is the Ambassador at the top, the Deputy Chief of Mission comes second, and then a myriad of section chiefs have the same rank, all answering to the DCM. Dan was the section chief for the security office. As I said, he was a nice enough fella, but didn't always do the right thing. He'd have to answer to the Ambassador as to why in the hell he didn't call the DCM right away to tell him that Gary just lost his shit and could be charged with a crime. But I wasn't about to keep this information under wraps, so I called the duty agent in the Office of Professional Management at headquarters.

The first thing the duty agent asked is whether I notified the DCM and, if not, why not?

"I suggested to Dan that I inform the DCM of the battery, and I told him that I'd contact OPR. He suggested I don't inform headquarters yet — that we should keep it quiet here at post. That's a bad idea, so that's why I'm passing this to you now," I told the duty agent who was responsible for these investigations at the headquarters level. "What do you want me to do?"

"Jesus, Alex. Dan told you not to tell *anyone*? Even OPR?"

"Yes, that's right."

"Well, it's a good thing you called. Can you send in a report in the next six hours?"

"Sure."

"Great, don't interview Gary yet." I'll let my Branch Chief know about this, but we need to see a report in the OPR inbox first thing in the morning. If it's not there, sorry to say it but you're going to get hammered by the RD. This sort of thing needs immediate action. Don't worry about Dan at this point, he doesn't seem to know how we handle these matters. FBI could potentially get involved and the Ambassador may eventually have to decide on whether to send Gary back to DC."

"Ok, what are my next steps?" I asked the duty agent, being certain that I follow the rules and do exactly what I'm told.

"The DCM needs to be notified ASAP. And I mean today, not Sunday. (The work week in Bangladesh was Sunday through Thursday). Let him know that I've already opened a DSS criminal investigation of Gary, and you need to interview Gary first thing Sunday morning." After a short pause, he continued. "Seriously, Alex. You need to follow these procedures. I had an ARSO in Burkina Faso last year who didn't report a sexual assault. He was removed from Post. The *Ambo* sent him back to DC. State doesn't mess around with these investigations. Tell Dan you spoke to me just to be on the safe side, and I told you that you must tell the DCM today. If he has an issue with it, call me and I'll have the RD reach out to him and un-ass his priorities."

I called Dan back after I hung up with headquarters and told him that DSS needs a report on the matter by 8:00 a.m. Washington time and that the OPR duty agent told me to inform the DCM about the incident immediately. Dan begrudgingly agreed to bring the DCM up to speed. I did as I was told and typed a report of investigation, or ROI, and sent it to DSS via email by 8:00 p.m. that day.

Sunday morning came too fast. But then again, I couldn't wait to get this assignment over with, so the faster it went, the better off I'd be. Besides, my family and I were taking our first R&R trip to Thailand next month. I couldn't wait to sleep through the night, eat Thai food, and clear my lungs. I spoke with the Ambassador about the events that took place in Gary's front yard, and he asked me what the next step of the DSS investigation was. Ambassadors are typically very intelligent people, of course, and my Ambo had been in the Foreign Service long enough as a career employee that he knew not to meddle in official investigations. I got along with him well, which was a nice benefit to have, especially in such austere conditions.

I called Gary into the conference room near my office and had a junior DSS Agent sit in on the interview and take notes. Having two people present during the interview not only ensures that nothing is missed, but also to have a note-taker do all the writing so the interrogator can concentrate on conducting the interview and not worry about taking notes. The lead agent asks the questions, the secondary agent takes all the notes. We're taught that at the police academy. Hell, I'd been through three academies with three different agencies in three different states, and they all teach interview techniques this way. That is why it was a surprise to see my secondary agent come into the conference room without a notepad or anything to write with. By this time, I already started interviewing Gary and didn't want to stop him mid-sentence, so when I had the chance, I just motioned to the secondary agent to write notes. He shook his head in disagreement, pointing to his head with his index finger and mouthed, "I got it."

After about forty-five minutes of interviewing Gary, I was satisfied with the information I had collected. Yes, he struck his gardener with a closed fist four or five times. Yes, he hit him because he wouldn't pick up dog poop in Gary's assigned residence. Yes, he understands this was wrong and he could be held accountable by State for battery. And yes, he'll inform his supervisor of the situation. I cut Gary loose and chatted with my Assistant RSO, who was supposed to be my note-taker.

"Why didn't you take notes?"

"Don't need to. I remember everything."

I was furious with him because note-takers are supposed to take notes *during* the interview, not after. This ensures that the information is put on paper immediately, and memory is not relied upon *after* the interview to jot down what was said *during* the interview.

"You know, we're taught that using a note-taker ensures that we don't miss anything, right? And if this case is taken up by OPR, they'll want to see notes from the interview."

"I'll write notes now, but I don't take them during the interview. I don't want messy notes, so I think about what I have to write, then I write it down after thinking about it."

"Well, that's not the correct procedure. You know that we are supposed to take notes during the interview and not rely upon memory when writing them later."

"Alex, I got an award from the Sheriff's Office for my excellent note-taking skills."

"But you're no longer a Sheriff's Deputy. Neither am I. We do this the DSS way. I get that you have some experience, man, but we all do. Dan was a Philly cop. Roger was Army Special Forces. I was a cop too, and Border Patrol Agent. We all have our past, but we need to do things the DSS way. That's the *only* way." He nodded in agreement, but the look on his face signaled to me that he didn't like going *by the book*.

Remember when I told you my father walked into Starbucks in Rosslyn and mentioned that all the guys there were full of themselves? Well, my ARSO was one of those guys. Fortunately, I had already been in Dhaka for a year and this guy just arrived. Now if I could only get through the second half of my tour without losing my shit.

I wrote my report and sent it back to DSS but also briefed the Ambassador on the situation. As I mentioned earlier, ambassadors are smart and know their role — not only as the top diplomat in the country they are serving, but also how to run an embassy. More importantly, if you're lucky, an ambassador will realize and admit that he or she doesn't know everything about security matters, in which case they ask for advice.

"What are my options, Alex?"

"Sir, you have two options. One is to keep Gary at post and hope that his gardener doesn't contact the police on this matter. If they do, that will damage my relationship with the Bangladeshi Police."

"The other option is to send Gary back to DC, essentially removing him from post because you've lost confidence in his ability to do his job properly. At that point, it becomes an HR matter, not a security issue. I can't guarantee that DSS will not pull his security clearance in the future but removing him from post because of a non-security matter is indeed an HR issue, which will likely not have such a bad effect on his career. Obviously, HR would know more about that than I do."

"Ok, what would you do in this situation, Alex?"

"Well, you could couch it like this: Give him an option to curtail from this assignment. I know he just arrived but giving him the option to leave his assignment before his two years is up wouldn't look bad on him. As we all know, Bangladesh is a very tough place to live and work, so no one would question his decision to curtail from this assignment. DSS still has an open investigation on him, but if you'd get him out of here, it wouldn't be detrimental to his career. I'm willing to bet if you agree to him leaving post, he'd take that option as opposed to being kicked out of post by an ambassador."

And that's exactly what the American Ambassador did. Gary submitted a request to State asking to leave the assignment early due to personal reasons, and it was approved. He was lucky, because not all ambassadors would allow this. As with every assignment, and every curtailment, there was usually more to it than meets the eye. Yes, someone might cut their assignment short and blame one thing — a sick mother in the States needed to be cared for, the kids were struggling in school, a spouse was homesick and wanted to be back home near family — but it also makes the ambassador look bad because every curtailment of assignment contains a possible element that the person leaving post didn't see eye to eye with a supervisor or the ambassador. In the security field, RSOs many times struggled maintaining their importance of protecting classified information, buildings, and people because a lot of the DCMs and ambassadors didn't care much about security. I struggled with this myself in my final overseas assignment, but not in this one.

Gary was in DC for a couple of months, then was reassigned to the American Embassy in Australia. The joke in my office was, if you don't like living in this hell hole, beat the crap out of someone, curtail from your assignment, and get reassigned to a great post in Australia. Well, that's the Foreign Circus, wrapped up in a nutshell.

In the meantime, the rest of us had to somehow get through two years in this shitty country and hope like hell someone on the Assignments Panel at headquarters would throw us a bone and send us to a nice post next.

* * *

As mentioned earlier, Bangladesh receives billions of dollars in foreign aid each year from governments and private sector corporations. One of these private entities is an American company which happens to be one of the richest and most profitable in the world. I received a call from a representative of the company who asked to meet with me in Dhaka to discuss aid grants for the Bangladeshi people.

A few weeks later, that rep flew to Dhaka, and we met at a restaurant near the embassy that I didn't think posed a real threat of being gunned down by Islamic extremists.

"Alex, I don't think one hundred percent of the financial investment my company sends to the people of Bangladesh makes it to its people. I'm concerned someone is siphoning some money out of the aid package we send to the government," the representative told me.

Well, I couldn't prove anything, and I was not in a position to make disparaging remarks about the country I was assigned to, but the chances that all the aid funding sent to Bangladesh makes it to the end user are slim to none.

The US Agency for International Development provided Bangladesh over two hundred million US taxpayer dollars in 2011 for emergency and humanitarian assistance, basic health projects, agriculture programs, government and civil society issues, education assistance, and energy as well as a slew of other initiatives. During a routine inspection and oversight of AID's spending, I spoke with the American federal Agent in Charge of conducting the audit in Bangladesh.

"Alex, I had an out brief this morning with the Ambassador about USAID spending in Sylhet, in northeastern Bangladesh."

"I've been there, sure. What did you find?"

"Well, in 2009, AID provided seven-hundred thousand US dollars to a pre-maternity care center that no one had seen before. It was supposed to be a brick-and-mortar operation complete with an MD, three nurses, lactation stations, and sonogram equipment. Well, when I arrived to conduct the inspection, it wasn't a center at all. It was a lean-to with a steel roof, dirt floor, no walls, no water, no equipment, no doctor, or nurses. There was a lightbulb dangling from the rafters. A few Bangladeshi ladies showed up and said they were running the place, but there was nothing — the care center didn't exist."

"That doesn't surprise me, Tony. In my humble opinion, USAID is wasting taxpayer dollars here. Hell, a dozen countries provide funding to Bangladesh and I'm willing to bet that less than ten percent of the aid reaches the end user. Most people are destitute, but the rich get richer."

I told Tony that I went to a cocktail party with my wife hosted by the Bangladeshi country manager for my contract security guard company, G4S. While he pays his employees peanuts for working at the American Embassy, he lives in a huge flat in the diplomatic enclave that is bigger and better than my house. When my wife and I arrived, we were met by a bunch of rich Bangladeshis, all of whom were driving BMWs and Mercedes Benz. The wives were dressed to the nines, the servants wore white gloves and were freely pouring Jack Daniel's, which you can't buy locally as it is a Muslim country. "The connected people here live like royalty. Whoever secured that USAID grant for seven-hundred thousand probably bought a nice house in Thailand with the money."

"I told the Ambo what I found," he told me, "and he said, 'AID is doing tremendous work here in Bangladesh.' He didn't want to hear about the seven-hundred grand."

I laughed. "No offense Tony, but AID should be phased out. It's the biggest waste of taxpayer dollars overseas that I can think of."

Getting tired of the foreign service lifestyle and the sacrifices I was making, and, more importantly, my wife and kids were making for my career, I grew weary of it all. I sat down for lunch one day with a government contractor in Dhaka who was on an assignment as a police mentor for the Bangladesh Rapid Action Battalion Police. Will McCarthy was a retired police chief from Alabama and had been hired under the International Criminal Investigator Training Assistance Program. He'd been in Dhaka for about a year.

"Will, I'm thinking about getting out. I just got over another bout with food poisoning, the international school sucks here, and I haven't slept through the night in months."

"How much time do you have left before you retire, Alex?"

"Nine years. I can retire in nine years."

"Want my advice?"

"Sure, what do you think?"

"Alex, I'd finish your career. Nine years will go by quick. At that point, you'll have your *fuck you* money and your pension, then you can go do whatever you want to do."

I remember that conversation like it was yesterday, and I'll never forget it. I followed Will's advice and decided that I'd stay in the State Department until I reached my twenty-year mark.

A couple months later, I was slated to take a trip with the US Ambassador and the Regional Director for the USAID to Rangamati in southeast Bangladesh. We were scheduled to depart the American Embassy in Dhaka later that night and drive to the airport to catch a flight to Chittagong, a beach town on the Bay of Bengal littered with plastic bottles and trash along the roads. I left work a bit early that day and walked five blocks to my house on 6th Avenue so I could eat dinner before walking back to the embassy to meet with the Ambassador and AID Director in the front lobby. By the time I left my house it was already dark, even though it was just before six o'clock in the evening.

The diplomatic enclave was the most expensive neighborhood in the entire country. Most of the foreign missions were located there and I could walk from the American Embassy to just about all of them. The Embassy of Canada was a block away, while the British High Commission was two blocks from my assigned house. Most of the streets were asphalt, but some were packed dirt. The sidewalks were made of six-inch slabs of concrete set over the top of deep concrete culverts, spanning from one edge to the other. The culverts were sewers, and occasionally, the concrete slabs were missing, leaving open sewers filled with wastewater from all the houses which emptied into a lake behind the neighborhood. One of the residents in the enclave once noticed a corpse floating in the lake, just a block away from my house.

As I walked down the dirt road, I decided to walk on the concrete sidewalk — the slabs of concrete covering the sewers — just to keep my shoes from getting too dusty. After all, I was meeting the Ambassador in a few minutes. Approaching an intersection, I crossed the street and headed toward the sidewalk. Because it was dark and streetlamps don't exist there, I noticed a dark patch of grass that I needed to cross before I reached the sidewalk. In an instant, I realized the rare patch of grass wasn't grass at all — it was the open sewer which didn't have a block of concrete covering the culvert ditch, and I fell into the dark, bacteria-laden shit water! Luckily, I reacted fast enough and braced myself on either side of the opening with my hands and arms, which stopped me from going fully under. And I am sure I would have, considering I couldn't feel the bottom with my feet, even though I was submerged up to my chest. I started heaving and coughing, and it was all I could do to stop myself from vomiting — the smell of the murky sewage water encompassing me. I'm not sure how deep that sewer was, but if I had hit my head on the edge of the concrete opening and knocked myself out, no one would have ever found me, not in a hundred years. The rats, with help from the nastiness and bacteria in the sewer, would have rotted my corpse to the point that DNA wouldn't have been recoverable. In that moment, I realized how lucky I got by not hitting my head on the culvert. As the saying goes, shit happens!

Mustering all my strength, I pulled myself out of the sewer as quickly as I could for fear that I'd either get eaten by some mutated creature or become infected from the bile I just fell into. Having been fortunate that I didn't get any of the water into my mouth or eyes, I wondered how stupid I could be to fall into an open sewer! But I didn't have much time to ponder this, as I still had a flight to catch, and I certainly couldn't go the way I was. I don't think my colleagues would appreciate the odor that accompanied my *new* appearance. I ran the few blocks back to my house and, upon reaching home, I took off my shoes and stripped off my slacks and Prada shirt, calling for my wife in the process. Wiping off my feet and body with a towel handed to me by our Muslim *ayi*, Anamika, who was shielding her face so she wouldn't see me naked, I then jumped into the shower for a thorough decontamination. Like clockwork at 6:00 p.m., the rolling blackout affected my neighborhood and I found myself once again washing my hair in complete darkness for ninety seconds before the generator in the front yard started, rattling the windows, and ensuring everyone had a whiff of diesel fuel.

"The most important thing is you didn't hurt yourself, honey," my wife said after I got cleaned up and put on fresh clothes.

"The bad news is, we'll have to throw out your shoes, suit, and the Prada shirt you bought in Rome. Not to mention, our Muslim housekeeper saw you completely naked when you took your clothes off in the foyer, so I think she is a bit shocked."

We both laughed a bit, and I wondered how I was lucky enough to meet such a beautiful Slovak woman who left her family and her country to follow me around the world to places like Bangladesh, while still having a sense of humor about the awful conditions in which we were raising our two young boys.

I made it back to the embassy just in time, and, as we were taking off for the trip to Rangamati, I told the Ambassador of my flirt with disaster and unwanted swim in the sewer. He gave me good advice, which had something to do with, "Be sure you walk on the streets. The sidewalks aren't always covered by slabs of concrete, and you could fall into the sewer." *Yeah, tell me something I don't already know.*

Somehow the two long years went by, and we found ourselves at the end of our assignment in Dhaka, which we loved and hated at the same time. Our youngest boy learned to walk and talk there, we met a lot of expats who we still keep in touch with, we traveled throughout

Southeast Asia which would not have been possible if we were assigned to DC, and my wife met Secretary Hillary Clinton when she visited the city and the American Embassy in 2012, just a few months before our departure. Still, we vowed never to return.

10
Seeing the Light

After serving two years in such a difficult place and doing a pretty good job while I was there, my bid list for my next assignment included a lot of European posts. But since I already served three years in Central Europe as the chief security officer, the likelihood that DSS would send me back to the region for another assignment was unlikely. So, it didn't surprise me when I was assigned yet again to the DSS Washington Field Office in Tysons Corner, Virginia. The last place I wanted to go — the last place *any* Foreign Service Officer or Specialist wants to go is headquarters. Our British friends were very happy for us because we were going to DC, but of course the last place they wanted to be posted was London. It goes both ways.

My wife had never lived in DC, even though she's traveled throughout the United States quite a bit even before we met, and she was equally disappointed that we weren't going to a nice overseas assignment like Norway, Brazil, or even Canada, ready for another adventure. But she quickly became to love everything the National Capital Region has to offer.

As far as assignments go, as much as I didn't want to go back to Washington, I realized it was nice to be back on the east coast, seeing friends again and eating good food. It was nice to watch college football on Saturday and not worry about food poisoning. But DSS was pushing all the special agents to serve at least one tour in a war zone such as Iraq or Afghanistan, places I hadn't ticked off yet during my career. Knowing I would have to do my part sooner or later, my wife and I made the decision that, after my tour in Washington, I'd volunteer for Iraq. It was the right time for me to go. Our kids were getting old enough to understand that Dad was not leaving them, and I knew Daniela was strong enough to handle things physically and emotionally.

I must admit, there was quite a bit of peer pressure to serve there and the likelihood of getting promoted would improve greatly if I volunteered. Besides, the money would be great. Consequently, I put a request in for a year in Iraq and bid on a position at the US Consulate in the southern Iraqi city of Basra, located twenty miles north of Kuwait and only eleven miles west of Iran.

Since we were renting a house in Vienna, Virginia, at the time, we agreed that while I'd attend Arabic language training and a tactical training course, my wife and kids would live in Fort Lauderdale. We bought a house not too far from the beach and moved from Virginia to Florida, then I returned to start my language course at the Foreign Service Institute in Arlington. Meanwhile, my wife had the unpleasant task of unpacking and getting the new house set up, getting the kids situated into new schools, finding new friends — pretty much getting our new lives figured out, on her own.

The training program that all DSS Agents must pass prior to going to a war zone is a brutal ten-week high threat operations course held in undisclosed locations. My wife didn't know where I was most of the time. We were trained in law, room-clearing and close quarter battles, off-road and high-speed driving, high threat dignitary protection, protecting high threat facilities, extensive firearms, defensive tactics, and so on. It was tough, even for an agent in great shape. As a class, we were kidnapped without being told in advance. While conducting a training exercise involving protecting a foreign dignitary, a group of the instructors threw frag grenades and shot us to hell without injuring any of us, put a burlap sack over our heads, and drove us to an undisclosed location somewhere in Northern Virginia. Eventually the sack was taken off and we were in some sort of warehouse, lined up against the wall in the dark. We were forced to take off our clothes and put on *thobes*, a long robe worn by Muslim men. We were then forced to recite scriptures from the Quran while our captors doused us with water from hoses. We stood for hours, reciting phrases we didn't know, listening to Arabic music blaring from speakers located in the adjacent room. We were cold and exhausted but had to push through. Finally, the next morning came, and the training exercise was over. The training was pretty good, but not terribly realistic. I supposed it was as close to being kidnapped without actually being kidnapped, so it served its purpose. It was Friday morning, and we were grateful to have the rest of the weekend off.

After completing the ten-week program, I returned to WFO to say goodbye to my supervisor and turn in my Chevy Impala before heading to my new home in Florida to see my wife and kids. We spent two weeks together, enjoying the warm weather and sunny beaches, before my flight departed Miami International, stopping in Amman and Baghdad, and finally landing in Basra, Iraq.

The US Consulate in Basra, before it was permanently closed by Congress, was located at the Basra International Airport. It was an eleven-acre compound surrounded by thirty-foot concrete walls and twenty-eight lookout towers. Over one thousand people lived and worked at the consulate, also known as an FOB, or forward operating base. Most employees only left the compound to take their R&R or when they completed their contract with the State Department. The compound had everything you really needed to live as comfortably as you could in the desert in a war zone — wi-fi, good food in the chow hall, a big fitness center, a pizza shop, coffee shop, snack shop, and a basketball court. For the money I was making, it wasn't too bad.

I met with the RSO, an experienced special agent named Mitch whom I liked immediately. Mitch showed me to my containerized housing unit, or CHU, where I'd live for the next year. A CHU is a steel shipping container just like the containers on a huge shipping vessel that transports goods from one country to another. I lived in one for a year, only mine looked like a small apartment inside. There was only one entrance, which was located near the end of the steel container. This end was my living room for the next year and had a sofa with a television which sat atop an old wood office desk, and a small refrigerator. The opposite end of the container was a double bed and nightstand. Separating the two ends was a small bathroom and shower.

Although we were in the desert, we rarely had hot water in the CHU, so I got used to taking cold showers.

On base, there were maybe thirty pods of containers. Each pod, or living area, contained sixty steel containers, stacked two-high. The pods were covered by a steel and metal roof which, in theory, would protect the containers from missiles or rocket-propelled grenades. I didn't want to test that theory.

Like many war zones, US Embassy personnel — both State Department folks, other government agency people as well as contractors — lived in steel shipping containers. On the American compound in Basra, there were several hundred security personnel. The guards in uniform were from Africa. The more experienced security folks were American security contractors and six DSS Special Agents, including me, to run the security operations.

Overall, it was a pretty good gig, although we worked six days per week. The only time anyone left the compound was to take a State Department employee into the local city to meet with someone, and most of those trips were useless. But the preparations for making these trips were time consuming, detailed, and expensive. When State requested DSS to provide security for the Public Affairs Officer, the security contract company called *Overwatch* would conduct a threat assessment, vulnerability assessment, and risk assessment of the location where the PA Officer wanted to go and brief the entire RSO team on the feasibility of making the movement without being attacked by Shia Muslims with close ties to the Quds Force in Iran. After receiving the RSO's approval, the team would get the armored vehicles ready to make the journey off the compound and into Basra. Armed with as much ammunition as we could carry, wearing protective body armor and Kevlar helmets, and ensuring our personnel tracking locator devices were working correctly, we ventured off the base with the PAO, who also wore body armor. Slow roll.

On a typical operation like this, we were armed with M-240 fully automatic machine guns that would shoot a 7.62-millimeter round, the M-249 squad automatic weapon, which was a bit lighter, and the M-4 carbine rifle as well as our 9-millimeter Sig Sauer pistols. Four vehicles, twelve fighters, and hundreds of rounds of ammunition, just to take the PAO to a local school simply to donate a dozen children's books. We'd risk our lives, and the life of that State Department employee, to try and promote freedom of speech, freedom of religion, and women's rights to mostly Shia Muslims who occupied Southern Iraq.

When the US led the invasion of Iraq in 2003, British soldiers paved the way from Kuwait to Basra, allowing American, Polish, and Australian troops the ability to continue to Baghdad. The Brits eventually pulled out of Southern Iraq and left their base for the United States, which became the US Consulate where I was assigned. The US was the last allied country to leave Southern Iraq, and eventually shut down the consulate for good in 2018 due to security concerns, according to Secretary of State Mike Pompeo. According to my own calculations, before it was permanently closed, the cost of operating the base exceeded one hundred million dollars per year, which means that it cost US taxpayers over four million dollars for the Public Affairs Officer to be taken to the school to just donate twelve books. This sounded like a waste of taxpayer dollars to me, and I think most Americans would certainly agree.

Life on the compound was, overall, pretty good. There was a massive cafeteria which served good food like steak, meatloaf, spaghetti, burgers, and salads for the Americans and Indian or Bangladeshi food for Africans. The workweek was Sunday through Thursday, but me and the other DSS Agents worked seven days per week, though we only worked a half day on Fridays. Each Friday night, the firefighters, all of them American, made pizza for dinner on their outdoor grill in their pod and invited some of the American security agents and contract guards over for a slice or two. It was a welcome reprieve from the sixteen-hour days of trying to protect the entire compound and was the highlight of my week.

Temperatures reached 140 degrees Fahrenheit during the summer months and some people took a rest and recuperation trip during these times to get out of the desert for a month, only to come back to the same boring routine on base which meant another ninety days of separation from the outside world until their next R&R. The internet connection was spotty at best, so we didn't have streaming music or streaming video to pass the time. The only thing to do on base to pass the time was to stay fit in the enormous gym or get together for a pick-up basketball game in the scorching heat, which nobody did. I recall spending a lot of time working out with the weights while the Kenyan security guards stayed fit by using the treadmills. Talk about guys that could run! While the rest of us Americans wore expensive cross training shoes, the Kenyans ran barefoot on the treadmills at a blazing pace of under four minutes per mile, while my fastest time was five minutes and forty seconds.

One Saturday morning, a mortar round was fired toward the base from a few miles away and landed just outside our compound near a vehicle entrance. I was on the phone with my wife at the time, a luxury which only occurred once or twice per week, when the sirens blared.

"Babe, I gotta go" I told her. "We might be getting attacked."
Click.

It was another twenty-four hours before I had a moment to call her back and let her know that I was OK. She must have been petrified, not knowing what had happened or whether I had been injured or even worse. *What the hell am I doing here? Why am I putting her through this?* I can't imagine what she was going through, not only then, but the entire time I was gone. We were inseparable at home. We did everything together. Some couples we know have nights *off* from one another to spend time apart, or even went on vacations without each other to take a break from the relationship, but that wasn't us. We wanted to be with each other and share moments together and with our kids, and I volunteered to deploy to the Middle East for our country. I wish that I had the luxury of *not* going, like my family. They were in Cincinnati, all of them. They had always gotten together for Christmas or Thanksgiving or birthday celebrations. They were there for each other and their families year after year. Watching football on the weekends, going to their favorite restaurants throughout the year, enjoying what they had and the life to which they had grown accustomed. But I had a different calling, one that drew me to help protect our nation, whether I was in the US or assigned overseas. Before my deployment to Iraq, my wife and kids and I visited my family and let them know that I was being assigned to Iraq. "Don't you like living in the US?" my older sister asked me.

What I wanted to say to her was, "I *love* living in the US. I love *having* what we *have* here. And that's why I'm going. To protect the lifestyle you're used to here." But I didn't. I just let the comment pass by, realizing she wouldn't understand, like most members of my family, that someone must protect our country from another 9/11 attack.

A few months later, my supervisor in Iraq was replaced with an agent originally assigned to replace me in the Washington Field Office but was instead offered and accepted the RSO position in Basra because another guy backed out of his assignment and left the position vacant. The new guy had some combat skills, but his interpersonal skills were virtually non-existent, making it extremely difficult to work with him, much less take orders from him. He was known for serving in one combat zone after another, without his wife, so I figured he either didn't want to be home with his wife, or his wife didn't want him home. I think he was assigned to Basra because DSS knew who he was and figured he couldn't operate in a *normal* embassy in a country that wasn't at war. Being a diplomat means you must get along very well with others and swallow your pride from time to time.

Moving around the world, especially with families to care for and spouse's career to compete with, meant that State Department employees changed their minds all the time. Most of us wanted to be overseas for most of our career. That's what attracted me to the job, but it's less of a career and more of a lifestyle.

I had a contractor work for me in the Tactical Operations Center in Basra who had been deployed for years. He had retired from the Marine Corp after twenty-nine years and decided to get on a security contract. I met him when I arrived. After about six months, he decided to go back home to Camp LeJeune, North Carolina, to continue his life with his wife and kids. He was hired by the Transportation and Safety Administration and was getting out of contract work once and for all. I wished him luck the day he left and hoped that he didn't miss Iraq or think about us who were still there. Four months later, I walked into the Operations Center and saw him getting a cup of coffee, chatting with the team! It turned out that he couldn't get by on his TSA salary, so he got back on the contract, making twice the amount TSA paid. It was blood money.

For me, the money wasn't worth being away from my wife and not seeing my boys grow up. So, I put in my required time, but I wasn't planning on staying any longer, or bidding on a war zone again. Coming to Iraq, I believed it was important and I wanted to do my part so that, one day, my boys wouldn't have to serve in a war zone. I wanted them to know that their dad served their country to make it better for them. But what I had hoped would be a rewarding time for me personally was more a heartfelt dissatisfaction with being a part of it all.

A few days before my tour ended, I had an out brief with the Consul General. Feigning interest in my thoughts about the tour in Basra, he asked me what I thought of the compound and whether I enjoyed my time there. *Really?* I thought to myself.

"Well, sir, to be completely honest, I can't get behind something that I don't think the US should be doing. I've followed orders and made a lot of money here, but I regret ever bidding on this assignment. In my humble opinion, we're wasting taxpayer dollars keeping the American flag standing in this desert. I met some great people here, and some assholes, and I'm glad to leave."

The next day my supervisor, Dickie Waters, who was one of those assholes, called me into his office.

"Alex, the CG told me that you did nothing but bitch about everything here."

"No, that's not true. I told him what I thought about the US Government's involvement in Southern Iraq. I also told him I regret bidding on this assignment. I know you've done nothing but shitty assignment after shitty assignment, but I think diplomacy is better served in a place *not* at war. You can have the war zone assignments because I won't bid on another."

"So, you think we should pull out of Iraq?"

"Congress has been contemplating pulling chalks for years. One day, they'll wise up and at least pull out of Basra."

"Well, Alex, the CG didn't think too much of your comments. What were you thinking?"

"Dickie, if the CG doesn't want to know the answer, he shouldn't ask the question. State put him in charge of this base, and he can't handle getting feedback? And he's a senior State Department employee? Having a guy like him, in charge of this base, goes to show how unimportant Basra is to Washington."

I was furious to be pinned down like that by a guy that I didn't respect and never liked. But that's DSS. Sometimes poor-performing employees are promoted and serve in positions that have quite an impact on US Foreign Policy. Every agency has them. DSS is no different. I couldn't wait to retire and wondered if I had five years in me to get through all the bullshit.

My one-year tour in Iraq went about as good as can be expected. Apart from the obvious — the money was great, and I was promoted while there, so I guess it was worth it. But it was not easy being away from home. My wife was dealing with everything on her own, raising the kids, dealing with the house, pool, cars, schools, and taxes. I was ready to leave Basra and had my sights on retirement. In the US Foreign Service, we can retire with a pension after twenty years of service and a minimum age of fifty.

But as it wasn't my time yet, and since I had already lasted this long, I submitted my bid list and hoped for the best. I wanted to be assigned to the Miami Field Office because we already owned a house in South Florida and my wife and kids were already well established there and enjoyed living near the beach. I certainly didn't want to be assigned to DC again and move everyone, yet again. Not many agents want to be assigned to Miami, so I was lucky enough to receive an email informing me that I got my top choice.

11
Back Home Again

My last day in Iraq was the best day I had in the past year, other than when I came home to visit my family for R&R. I said goodbye to some folks, tossed my duffel bag into the back of an armored van, and drove five hundred yards to the airbase that I had protected over the last six months. The CIA plane which just arrived from Baghdad landed and the crew opened the doors. A small group of people got out. Some of them I knew. They were returning from their R&R trip. Some I didn't. Those folks were arriving at the base to begin their one-year tour. *Poor bastards.*

"Alex, you out of here for good?" a contractor who worked for me in the Operations Center asked.

"10-7, my brother. Headed home."

"Where's your next assignment?" he asked as I walked to the small aircraft.

"Miami."

"Fuck you," he said, smiling. "Enjoy being home."

I flashed the peace sign, walked up a few steps and disappeared into the plane.

For the first time in my career, I didn't have to move before starting a new assignment. I simply arrived at home, dropping my bags in the foyer of our beautiful house, which was a new construction when we bought it the previous year. No boxes to unpack or pictures to hang, no closets to organize or furniture to put together. No trips to Costco to load up on groceries. I got home to music playing and candles burning, while delicious wafts of garlic and other aromas of a home-cooked meal carried from the kitchen. My beautiful wife was waiting for me with open arms, our kids bouncing up and down around her. I pulled them all into a group hug, squeezing hard, relishing in the moment. As the boys fired their questions, I tried to describe what it was like living in Southern Iraq, hearing the local tribes shoot rocket propelled grenades at each other during disputes. Although I had lived in four other countries before I was deployed to Iraq, I was fascinated by how the residents in Basra lived and carried on with their days amidst the warring tribes just outside of town, the presence of the Iranian Quds Force eleven miles to the east across the border in Iran, and the lack of drinking water, lack of schools, and the absence of sustainable food. My kids enjoyed hearing about the enormous camel spider I saw on the tarmac of the airfield. This spider was twelve inches in diameter and stood over seven inches tall! When I spotted it near the airplane hangar, I alerted the local Iraqi security guard there to help me protect the airfield. He grabbed a broom and chased the spider from one end of the hangar to the other before he finally killed it.

After a customary few weeks off work between assignments, my new supervisor picked me up at six in the morning and we drove an hour south into Miami-Dade County, arrived at the office at seven, and he handed me keys to my government ride, a black Dodge Charger. We had worked together years earlier in DC, working on protective security details of Secretary of State Condoleezza Rice and John Kerry. He was also on the protective detail of Hillary Clinton when she visited Bangladesh a few years prior.

"Eddie, do you remember the guy who worked in OGA in Bangladesh?" I asked. "Big dude, worked with me on a couple CT matters when you were there with Clinton."

"Yeah, what was his name?"

"Forrest, I think."

"Yep, I remember him. What about him?"

"He's in prison. Convicted of having sex with women while he was in Bangladesh and filming it without them knowing he was taping it."

"Jesus! Seriously?"

"Allegedly, he slipped a Roofie into the drinks of some women and raped them. Sorry, *non-consensual* sex."

176

Roofie, or Rohypnol, is a drug that incapacitates a person rendering impaired cognitive functions. It's commonly known as the date-rape drug.

"Not sure how many and I'm not sure if the girls were locals, or expats, or what. Maybe some worked at the American Embassy, I'm not sure."

"Holy shit! The Foreign Service is full of weirdos, most of whom probably can't hold down a decent job in the US but lucked out when they passed the Foreign Service Exam."

* * *

After a few months of working criminal investigations in the South Florida area as a Branch Chief, supervising a team of six Special Agents, I was assigned to the protective detail of Prince Harry, Duke of Sussex. He was coming to South Florida to play polo in a charity event. After the fundraiser, we were scheduled to drive him to Disney World for an appearance at the 2016 Invictus Games, an international multi-sport event founded by Harry to honor the mental and physical achievements of wounded and injured armed forces personnel — both serving and veterans.

DSS Headquarters assigned me as the Tactical Commander for the South Florida portion of the detail. Once in Orlando, I was to hand that position off to another DSS Agent. In setting up my security team, I selected agents whom I'd already worked with and who I could trust to be on time, be professional, and look sharp. I assembled a solid group to handle the arrival of Prince Harry at Miami International Airport and to take him to West Palm Beach for the charity event at a private polo club to raise money for his foundation. Although I was not going to be a part of the security team while at Disney World, agents needed to be scheduled to protect the Prince while he was in public and to watch his hotel room or house, wherever he stayed, twenty-four hours per day until he departed back to England, and it was my responsibility to make the schedule.

The State Department in general, and DSS specifically, makes no effort in hiding the fact a diverse workforce represents American ideals abroad. In the US, while working a protective security detail, the managers in the field offices around the country have a goal in putting the best agents on a protective detail, especially on a high-profile VIP like the one we were preparing for in Miami. The problem with this is no one wants a discrimination complaint filed against them, especially by a member of a minority group. DSS Agent positions are mainly filled by white males, and I have every bit of respect for a woman to get selected for a career with DSS, complete all the training, endure the extensive travel, and win the respect of her peers who may have much more experience in the military or previous law enforcement careers. Most women in DSS have done so. A few have not, although they may have had their chance to prove they are capable of difficult assignments, both domestically and abroad. My colleague was on this list.

Karina Raleigh was a big woman, seemed somewhat smart, and was an average supervisor and leader. I didn't trust her, but I never heard her team complain about her. Well, to be fair, a male DSS Agent complaining about a female agent is something that would most likely lead to the female agent filing a discrimination case with the Office of Equal Employment Opportunity and the male agent would be branded as having done something wrong. It could ruin one's career and will most certainly ruin their assignment in that office. My colleagues and I were at a meeting at headquarters a few years earlier, and a very senior DSS Agent told a group of us that the agency aims to promote black women, white women, and Asian women at a much faster rate than white men. After the meeting was over and everyone started making their way out of the conference room, an Asian female agent who didn't have a great reputation in DSS walked past and said, "Looks like you're screwed," with a smirk on her face. That year, she was promoted. And that's the way it is, not only in DSS but in State in general.

I'd gotten along with Karina, whom I outranked. The Agent in Charge of the Field Office as well as DSS Headquarters gave me the freedom to assign agents to the Prince Harry detail if they were available. Given that field agents from the Miami Field Office were regularly tasked with temporary assignments conducting missions overseas, my choices were limited. We needed to fill the role of a supervisor to work midnight shift at Disney World. Karina was the only supervisor available, so I assigned her, and sent my staffing pattern to headquarters, ensuring that MFO had things under control and were ready for the security detail. She had other ideas.

First, allow me to set the tone: Karina had never served in a war zone and openly told anyone who happened to be paying attention that she wasn't going to serve in a war zone, no matter what headquarters said. In fact, she refused to enroll in the high-level operations course all agents were required to take. She simply refused. And she got away with it. Senior administrators at headquarters let her refuse to do her job or take training, and yet she was still getting promoted faster than the men who had a better track record and showed more capability to be an agent.

After notifying all the agents assigned to the Prince Harry detail, she walked into my office.

"Alex, I see you assigned me as the *Mids Shift Leader* in Orlando."

I looked up. "Hi, Karina. Yes, I've got you down as a supervisor at Disney resort. We needed a supervisor to work midnights up there. It should be quiet. Nice hotel, easy work," I replied.

"Yeah, I'm not working midnights," she said curtly.

"Well, we are using a lot of junior agents during days and swings, and we really need an agent on mids that has some solid experience, so I've got to put you down for that position, sorry. HQ has already agreed to the staffing pattern, and we don't want to put someone right out of the academy into that slot."

"Well, find someone else for it. I really don't want to go to Orlando for this detail anyway, and be away from my family for two nights, and I'm a mother, so working a different shift just isn't going to work for me."

Here we go. I had a feeling this would be a problem.

"Uh, well I'll ask my supervisor to see if there is someone else available to take your spot on this detail."

"I can work the detail, but I won't work mids."

"Ok, so you *are* available to work the detail and go to Orlando?"

"Sure, but I'm not working mids."

"Karina, I'm sorry but the Ivory Tower in Rosslyn isn't going to allow an FS-03 to be the shift leader up there. You're a junior FS-02, so I don't have much choice unless headquarters wants to send down an FS-02 to fill the role you don't want." I attempted to explain, diplomatically and with kid gloves, that the Ivory Tower — DSS Headquarters — wants and needs her working midnight shift.

"Alex, if you don't put me on day shift, I'm going to call Brett at headquarters about it."

Brett was the agent in the Office of Dignitary Protection which was responsible for coordinating with foreign governments and their security details of foreign dignitaries traveling to the United States. When DP sends out a tasker to a Field Office, they don't *ask* us to devise a workable security plan for the protection of a foreign dignitary, they *tell* us to do it. I was being directed by DP to staff the detail with agents, and an FS-02 supervisor would work the midnight shift. Karina was the only FS-02 available.

Staffing a security detail is usually simple. Most agents want to get out of the office, work a fun detail like the one coming up, and make some good money. I wasn't sure why she was so hung up on working the midnight shift, but I spoke to the MFO Agent in Charge.

"Brooks, I've run into a snafu while staffing this Prince Harry detail."

The last thing that a boss wants to hear is that one of his subordinates has a problem, especially if he doesn't offer a solution to the problem.

"Alex, we're in Miami. Look outside," he said, motioning toward the glass wall in his corner office overlooking Biscayne Bay. "There are no problems here."

I explained that Karina, in no uncertain terms, refuses to work midnight shift at Disney World during the Duke of Sussex detail. We went back and forth as to who we could get to replace her but nobody else was available.

"She said if I don't take her off mids and put her on days, she'd call headquarters. I'll let Brett know about this before it blows up, but you and I may have an EEOC complaint filed against us if she is so inclined — and you know she has a track record of being untrustworthy and spreading rumors, and I wouldn't put it past her to contact the Office of Civil Rights over this. She mentioned that, since she is a mother, she can't work the midnight shift. I've never heard that excuse before, so who knows what she is capable of claiming."

Brooks thought about if for a minute. He certainly didn't want to be accused of doing anything wrong that would rise to the attention of HQ or the Office of Civil Rights. Hell, he was due to retire soon and had no intention of risking his reputation, although he and I had done nothing wrong. And I didn't blame him. We were both cornered by a female who had a gripe and was using her gender to get what she wanted. In the private sector, this sort of matter may not be very common, but in the State Department, threatening a coworker or supervisor with contacting OCR was always on the table, and used with frequency.

"Alex, do whatever she wants."

And that was that. The organization had gone off the rails. A female agent who refused to take the best training and refused to leave her family for an assignment in a war zone — like we all had to do at some point — looked me in the eye and threatened that she would file a complaint with headquarters if I didn't take her off midnight shift, on a detail that lasted three days. Not only had I grown to despise the State Department, but the condemnation I had for DSS had just boiled over. Retirement couldn't come fast enough. I had four years to go before I could leave it all behind.

To say there are a lot of privileges that come with being a British Prince is an understatement. While doing some advance work a few days before the security detail began, I conducted a walkthrough of a mansion on the island of Palm Beach, Florida, just a few hundred yards away from former President Trump's estate. It was in this house that one of several fundraisers would be held in honor of Prince Harry's visit to the US. As I walked the property with the grandson of the owner, inspecting the rooms where the gala would be held, the back yard and the beachfront, the powder rooms the Prince might use, and the multiple exits out of the house and off the property, both by vehicle motorcade and by boat, we met the homeowner. She was a lovely old woman whose husband was a real estate mogul and had years ago passed on. We stood in the grand room where she explained when and where she would greet the Prince when he arrived for the event. As I looked around the room, I noticed the huge fireplace and the paintings on the wall.

"Is that a Picasso above the fireplace?" I asked, studying the large abstract painting of a group of naked women with contorted bodies and eyes that seem to look right at you wherever you stood.

"Not only is that Picasso's work *above* the fireplace," the antique homeowner replied, "but on *either side*, too."

I hadn't noticed the two smaller paintings because my gaze was drawn to the odd-looking painting over the mantle that *must have been* a Picasso. The paintings on either side of the fireplace were of horses in meadows.

"People know him for his cubism and impressionism work, but he also painted landscapes," the old lady said, smiling.

In a house worth some fifty million dollars, soon to host Prince Harry for a fundraiser, most definitely the paintings were authentic works of art. I wondered how much had been invested in just those three pieces alone, and how many more there were throughout the eight-bedroom, twelve-bathroom French-style home sitting on the Atlantic. *And I thought I had it good.*

As the grandson, a guy younger than I by about ten years, showed me the dining room and kitchen, I asked to go onto the rear patio facing the extensive yard and ocean. We walked through a butler's pantry where an older gentleman, very tan and fit, was seated at the breakfast table having a cup of coffee and reading the newspaper. Seconds later as we exited onto the patio I turned to the grandson, a recognizable expression of surprise on my face.

"Pete, was that George Hamilton?" I asked, inquiring if the man having coffee was the American actor who has been in notable films including *Zorro, Love at First Bite, The Godfather, and Doc Hollywood.*

"Uh, yeah. He and my grandmother have had a thing going on for a long time."

A few days later, I put on a blue suit and my earpiece, enlisted the assistance of a Miami Airport uniformed police officer, and met the Prince as he got off the plane at Miami International.

We picked him up and drove him to West Palm Beach where he would spend the night before going to a private club to play in a polo match. I've done some interesting things in my career and watching Prince Harry play in a polo match in South Florida was definitely one of them. Afterwards, a fundraiser held at the horse stables had gone off without a hitch and with the official part being concluded, the younger crowd stayed behind to listen to music and party. My team and I waited by the vehicles a hundred yards or so away, next to the motorcade, to give the VIP his space. We were on a privately-owned estate and polo grounds with plenty of armed security at the entrances and around the perimeter. The media was gone, the fundraiser was over, and most of the guests left. We could relax a bit.

As all details tend to go, agents work long hours without a proper break, always on the go. When we get a chance like this, we reach into the back of the armored Tahoe for an energy bar and energy drink and shoot the shit, enjoying the rare downtime. One of the guys on my team, Marko, started talking about the time we worked on Secretary Kerry's detail in Berlin. Agent Morelli was the Agent in Charge of the detail, and I was the limo driver.

"Did you hear what happened to Morelli?" Marko asked, his eyebrows raised.

"He got on as the Chief Security Officer for the Miami Heat?" I asked.

"No, dude. He got arrested."

"What?" For what!?"

"Something about indecent liberties with a minor," Marko replied.

"What? Like sexual assault?" I asked.

"No, it's worse than that. Rape."

As it turned out, the criminal case against Morelli was later dropped. I've heard and read a lot of cloak and dagger stories about Morelli and the CIA, connections with the Chicago Mafia and the Vatican. I've heard about the Benghazi attacks and Hillary Clinton's involvement and how Morelli was a very influential man, not only in DSS but even the upper echelons of the US Government. That's a story for another time. The Duke of Sussex was walking toward our motorcade.

"Prince, what can we do for you?" I asked Prince Harry as he approached us from the stables.

"I need another shirt. Is my bag in the back of the Cadillac?"

"It's in the Tahoe. Marko, can you crack the seal on the back hatch?"

"What happened to your shirt, Prince?" I asked.

"Someone spilled wine on it."

"Well, was she pretty, at least?"

"It was some guy!" he said, exasperated, yet laughing.

"Oh man, what are you doing?" I laughed, as if to say what the hell is a guy doing close enough to you to spill wine on your shirt. *You're a goddamn Prince, for heaven's sake!* The Duke of Sussex laughed, changed his shirt in the private drive, and walked back across the lawn to the horse stables and party.

Although I didn't get to know him very well, I know that he's very likable and approachable. He doesn't have an air about him that one would think famous people, or royals, have. Whenever he visited the US, one of the first stops he'd want to make is Five Guys for a hamburger. I remember thinking that it would be nice if he were a US Senator or Congressman; we need someone like him at the highest levels of government.

The next morning, we left for Orlando and Disney World, ninety minutes to the north. When we arrived, the motorcade pulled up to the entrance at the hotel where Prince Harry was staying, and the detail agents formed a loose diamond formation around him, escorting him to his suite. A DSS Command Center had been established in a nearby hotel room and was equipped with weapons, extra radios and batteries, maps, bottled water, a base radio, and a supervisor who was responsible for ensuring the hotel security team didn't allow anyone into his room and protected the Prince while he was in the hotel. Now that we arrived in Orlando, my responsibilities for the security detail were over. My team and I drove back to Miami while Karina, who was the dayshift supervisor for Disney World, along with her team of agents, assumed responsibilities for the remainder of the detail.

A few days later, back in the Miami Field Office, I met with a few of the agents on the detail to discuss what went right, what went wrong, and how we could have done a better job protecting our VIP. When I asked how things went in Orlando, one of my men told me the reason Karina didn't want to work the midnight shift.

"Sir, she wanted to work dayshift because her husband and kids were in Orlando with her. She got off each day at 5:00 p.m. and enjoyed the amusement parks after work with her family. What's more, she used her credentials to get everyone in for free!"

Wow, so a female agent threatens a male agent to work a specific shift just to get her and her family into Disney World by using her official position as a Special Agent for personal gain. I passed this information along to my supervisor in Miami as well as Brett at headquarters.

"Watch your back," I warned Brooks. "I don't want to work with that woman ever again."

DSS had gotten to the point where men didn't want to work with women out of fear they would file a complaint if they were not happy with something, with anything. Most of these complaints were completely unfounded, and everyone knew it, but an allegation in DSS means you're guilty until proven innocent, not the other way around. I had four more years before I could retire, and I didn't know if I could make it to the end.

It was time for me to bid again. Two years in Miami was stressful enough, although it should not have been, and I was ready to leave. But even if I wasn't, I had no choice. That was the career I chose — moving from one assignment to the next.

"One more tour overseas," I said to my wife. "Are you up for it?"

Another tour in Iraq certainly wasn't an option for my family. Being away from home for another year was out of the question. It was time to learn a new language and go somewhere interesting, so I bid on posts in Southeast Asia. Eventually, I received a call from headquarters.

"Alex, you have a solid reputation in DSS, and we'd like for you to be the RSO in a post in China. Would you rather go to Shanghai or to Guangzhou?"

"Well, thanks for the offer, sir. I certainly appreciate the choices. I haven't been to either place. What do you suggest?"

"Personally, I like Guangzhou better. That's where I'd go. It's a great family post, great Consulate."

A few days later, I received an official notification that I was assigned as the RSO, or head of security, at the American Consulate in Guangzhou, China. Some assignments in the Foreign Service require an agent to learn the language before going to a non-English speaking country. China is one of them. I enrolled in a one-year language course at the Foreign Service Institute in Arlington, Virginia, just outside of DC. *This should be interesting,* I thought to myself. A year away from DSS, in school to learn a new language at US Government expense. Sounds great!

Unfortunately, we had to move again. Well, my wife and kids could have remained in our house in Fort Lauderdale while I attended training in the national capital region, but we didn't want to be separated again. So, we sold our house and were getting ready to move into an apartment near the training institute, which was like a small college campus where a lot of classroom-type training was conducted for State Department personnel. We sent the kids to my wife's parents' home in Slovakia for six weeks while we sorted through our belongings, deciding what would go where. This was one of the more difficult moves as far as the packing went. We had to set aside things we would take with us for the upcoming year in Northern Virginia, then divide the rest into two piles. Well, more than piles. First was household items and furniture that would remain in a storage facility in Maryland until we completed our assignment in China. The remainder were other necessities and extra clothing that would be shipped to a storage facility in Antwerp, Belgium, for a year and would eventually be delivered to us in China after my language training was over. A total nightmare. But we managed, as we always do, and after a couple of weeks we were done with the movers, the house was clean and we just loaded the last of our belongings into our two cars, ready to drive north. Well, not just yet, first we needed a little time to relax. We checked into a beachfront hotel, thinking the worst part of this move was behind us.

Three days before driving to DC from Florida, I suddenly woke up in the middle of the night, feeling a pain in my chest and shooting down my right arm. As I tried to keep calm and steady my breathing, hoping it would pass, I had different scenarios running through my mind. Minutes passed and I started panicking, cold sweat forming on my chest as my breath grew shallower. I rolled over and gently shook my wife's arm to wake her up. "Babe, I think I'm having a stroke. Or a heart attack. I'm not sure, but something is wrong."

"What?! Let's get you to the hospital!"

Upon our arrival at Fort Lauderdale Hospital in the middle of the night, the staff, and later doctors, didn't seem to care too much that I had been admitted at the ER. Having explained that I was in terrible pain and scared as hell about what I was going through, I was left waiting in the reception area for over two hours. They simply forgot that I was there. When I was finally ushered into one of the examination rooms, I answered some basic questions before I was examined by a nurse. At last, a doctor came in to *take a look*. To my obvious dislike, everybody was moving at a very slow pace and concluded with a lack of any diagnosis on their part, suggesting there is nothing wrong with me.

"Mr. Reinshagen, everything appears to be normal, all your vital signs seem fine. I recommend you have an EKG done," came from the doctor.

"I can assure you that I'm not fine right now," I snapped back.

"Sir, we can't do anything for you unless you have an EKG done. If you don't want to have that done, there is no reason for you to be here. We can't find anything wrong with you."

"If I may — and I know I'm not an expert — but based on my husband's symptoms and the bumps on the back of his head, I think he might have Shingles. Don't you think that might be the case?" came from my wife hovering over me, concerned that I was in pain, and afraid.

As you can imagine, my wife's suggestion was not received well, the arrogant doctor smirking down on her, saying it's not Shingles. We left the hospital after wasting several hours there and came away with no information about my health. The sun was rising as we got back to the hotel, and I tried to get some rest but couldn't. I was anxious about our upcoming drive north and how would I handle it in this state.

"Babe, I honestly think it might be Shingles. But whatever it is, we need to get a second opinion. We need to figure this out and get you better, fast. There is a twenty-four-hour emergency care place in one of the shopping plazas nearby," said my ever-so-caring wife to me after I got out of bed, giving up on sleep.

After I showered and got dressed, my wife drove me to the emergency care facility, and we once again explained my symptoms to the doctor on duty.

"Well, Alex, I suggest you have an MRI done on your head, but we don't do that here. You'd have to go back to the hospital to get that done. They are pretty backed up so it will probably be a month or so before you can get in."

"Ah, a month? I'm in some real pain here, so I really can't wait a month. Besides, we are moving to DC the day after tomorrow. Is there anything else you suggest I do? My wife thinks it might be Shingles..."

"Hmm, it crossed my mind that you could have Shingles, but you're way too young for that so I'm certain you don't. There is a good doctor in Deerfield Beach who specializes in neurology, so maybe you could see him."

Daniela called Dr. Winters and, luckily, was able to get me an appointment first thing in the morning of the next day. My pain was not receding, and I was growing more and more worried by the minute. I hadn't slept much, my body aching, and my skin very sensitive to the touch. The next morning couldn't come soon enough. We made the thirty-minute drive north and were greeted by an older gentleman as soon as we entered the offices, the doctor was expecting us. After meeting with him for just a couple of minutes, he said, "Special Agent Reinshagen, it's very unusual. You're young, in excellent condition, and you have Shingles."

She was right. I saw two doctors including one in a hospital ER and neither of them knew what was wrong. My wife knew I had Shingles, though. Doc handed me a prescription for a medication, and we left his office in a hurry to get it filled at a nearby pharmacy. Twenty minutes later, my wife handed me the first dose. As she started pulling out of the parking lot of the pharmacy, I took the pills, eager for the pain to stop, and spent the rest of the day, and most of the next one, in bed, finally starting to feel some relief. In the end I was able to manage the sixteen-hour drive to DC.

It seems the stress of moving again, selling our home, and starting over, combined with my weakened immune system after a major back surgery I had just a few months prior, left me vulnerable. Perhaps, the bumps on the back of my head were concealed by my hair and made the diagnosis difficult, I kept telling myself after this miserable experience. Doctor Winters noted I was lucky we caught it before the Shingles virus could spread to my face. I was indeed very grateful for that, even though it seemed I've had a lot of obstacles thrown my way lately. The spine fusion surgery I had undergone after returning from my tour in Iraq was long and painful, and the two-year recovery was brutal. I was rendered completely dependent on my wife for everything

— getting up from bed, getting dressed, helping me in the shower; I needed help doing everything I had always taken for granted. It took me several weeks before I could walk on my own, without the aid of a walker. As they say, everything comes in threes, so I hoped this was it for me. My wife got me through a shoulder surgery, back surgery, and now Shingles.

* * *

I was really looking forward to learning a new language — my fourth foreign language. My Arabic language skills were quite rusty, however, and my Slovak language skills were slowly disappearing, too, but my Spanish was solid, and I was ready to tackle Mandarin. The first few days, it was a slow-moving class. My head was buzzing from the *meds* I was still taking, as the class started with the basics — just like a child in China would learn how to speak, we did also. I'd arrive for class at eight in the morning and we would only speak and read Mandarin. After class, I'd have a couple hours of homework each night. I'd study on weekends, and it was tough! But after a few months, I could hold a conversation in Chinese. After a few more months, my wife told me I would talk in my sleep in Mandarin, although she had no idea what I was saying. And after a few more months, I was dreaming in the Mandarin language — conversations in my dreams were all in Chinese. That's what intensive eleven months of language training will do.

The course was not only about learning the language, but also about learning the Chinese culture. We were immersed in the familial hierarchy, the politics, education system, and the food. Yes, I suppose it sounds fun, doesn't it? After a year of it, by the time the course had ended, I was so sick of it all that I had my doubts that I even wanted to go to China, but that feeling wore off and we packed our things yet again.

Three years in China would take me to retirement, I figured. *This is my last assignment in DSS.* The plan was that we'd return to DC after this assignment, and I'd find something else to do in retirement. We bought a house in Northern Virginia and rented it out just a few weeks before we left the US for Southeast Asia, excited to return to it and grow roots near our friends.

12
The Wuhan Virus

One of the difficulties with being in the Foreign Service, aside from moving around the world every two or three years, is moving around the world with your family, and your pets. We had planned this move for months — the school records and registration in China, our medical vaccinations for yellow fever and typhoid, preparing my SUV for three years of storage in Maryland, language training, financial preparation, the diplomatic visas for China, and the huge amount of paperwork we needed to have our dog on the flight with us from Reagan National Airport in Arlington, Virginia.

We arrived at Reagan International Airport for an early morning departure with all our bags and our dog, Jewel, in her crate. I liked flying out of Reagan as opposed to Dulles International. It was much smaller than Dulles, easier to navigate through security checkpoints and terminals, and wasn't as busy. We had the visas, and the plethora of airline and TSA authorizations and paperwork for Jewel to get her not only on the plane but also to ensure she clears customs in China. It had been just about one year since we moved out of Florida, and now were moving out of Virginia, flying to a city we had never visited. We were still groggy from getting up in the middle of the night, but anxious nevertheless to travel twelve time zones to the opposite side of the earth. Unfortunately, as we stepped up to the check-in counter, United Airlines delivered us the bad news.

"Sir, your pet isn't cleared for this flight," the United Airlines agent informed us.

"What? Sure, she is. I paid for her ticket, here's the receipt and the authorization letter stating we can put her on the flight."

"Yes, sir. I see that, but you're flying to Guangzhou where the tarmac temperature at this time of year exceeds a 120 degrees

Fahrenheit. We don't allow pets on the flight when the temperature at the final destination is above eighty-five degrees." She continued, "you'll have to wait maybe three or four months to bring your pet with you."

I was getting livid. We hadn't even started travelling and we already had a major problem.

"What are you talking about? We're moving to China. Today. We can't wait three months. I have a job to get to."

"Yes, I understand, but we're not putting your dog on this aircraft."

An argument ensued, and my temper skyrocketed. Months of planning had been completed for this day. My wife, Daniela, had to step in and calm my obvious but justified rising impatience before I tore the airport down. I went from angry to desperate to pretty much giving up in just a few minutes. Resigned, I stepped aside to make a phone call to our travel agent while she went in search of another employee, hoping we might get a different response. Somehow, as she always does, she spoke to another airline representative and got us and our dog on the flight. She's very good at getting what she wants. It seems she always gets what she wants and, for years, I attributed this to her looks — beautiful face, stunning blue eyes, and long brown hair. I learned, though, it was not intentional on her part and that people were just naturally drawn to her the same way I was. When dealing with men, she got anything she asked for. Hell, I'd cut off half my finger if she asked me to. But she's also able to get things done and get what she wants when talking to women too, including the airlines supervisor. Her way of communicating with others is impressive, and that's something I have never mastered.

She convinced the airlines that we had everything we were required to have to get our dog on the flight — the kennel, paperwork, vaccinations, approval from the Chinese Government and American Embassy in Beijing — and calmly asked if there was anything at all they could do for us. The only way around the *heat policy* was to split our flight reservations into two separate flights as opposed to treating it like one flight with a layover. In that case, United Airlines would be only responsible for the first portion of the flight and would allow us on the plane to JFK, where we would have to collect our dog and all our bags and re-check everything for the second flight. As much as it seemed like a huge headache, it was our only option at this point, so my wife thanked the nice lady helping her and told her to proceed with whatever she needed to do. We were fortunate the airline representative was willing to go to those measures for us.

"Ma'am, I don't see your reservation here anymore. That's really odd."

"What?? That can't be right!" Daniela responded, wondering what else could go wrong.

"What's going on?" I asked as I stepped up to the counter again after finishing my phone call.

"This wonderful lady found a way to get us on the plane, I'll explain the details later, but we'll have to re-check Jewel and all our bags in New York. But now she can't see our reservations anymore..."

"Well, I just cancelled our flights, thinking we..."

"Are you serious?! Why would you do that??" my wife said with a raised voice before I could even finish my sentence.

"I didn't think we would be able to get on that plane, so I called the travel agency's after-hours number to let them know," I stated, annoyed with myself for acting on a whim but mainly still very angry with the previous United agent.

"Call back right now and get us on that plane again!"

Luckily, with only minutes to spare, running through the airport, we all made it on the flight to JFK. As we settled into our seats, I squeezed my wife's hand tightly, unable to speak, relief spreading through my body. Our son was crying, worried about Jewel, as we had to leave her in a rush. At last, we all calmed down and mentally readied ourselves for what was to come, hoping we would not run into any more problems at JFK.

To our dismay, the nightmare was not over yet. Rushing through the terminal at Kennedy International, we were thankful to find Jewel waiting for us in her crate at the exact spot they said she would. But there was a problem with getting on the next flight, and this time not because of Jewel — China Southern Airlines was not worried about her — but because our flights were separated. To this day, I'm not exactly sure what the problem was — something to do with the second flight not being under the same reservation number as the first. After a long back-and-forth between the airline representative and person from the travel agency on the phone, we were able to have it resolved and made our connecting flight. In that moment I vowed I would never put my family through something like this ever again.

We were on finally our flight. *Guangzhou, here we come!*

Once we arrived in Guangzhou, we collected our baggage and the dog crate with Jewel — she made the trip in good spirits. We were assigned a magnificent apartment in the affluent neighborhood not far from the US Consulate, and everything seemed like it would be a great assignment. It was late July 2018.

After a few weeks of living and working as diplomats, it was abundantly clear to us that we, the Americans, were vigorously despised by the Chinese people. The Chinese Government had spied on us and others in the expat community to the point they didn't even hide what they were doing. When we were out of our apartment, they'd enter it and tamper with our electronics. They would move objects just to let us know they had control over us, control of our things, and control of what happened to us while we lived there. To make matters worse, relations between Washington and Beijing had always been tenuous, but lately, they were worsening.

Despite the constant stares from the locals, life in China was interesting, to say the least. The downtown area of Guangzhou is an ultra-modern city with high rise buildings made of steel and glass, expensive restaurants, and five-star hotels. It was quite an impressive sight, one that I really didn't expect. Venturing outside the business district, however, it was apparent the city was bifurcated into the *haves* and the *have nots*. Visits to the local *wet market* and food shops were a better experience than in Bangladesh, although the Chinese snickered at us on most occasions when we attempted to speak the local language. It was then that I realized the eleven months I spent learning to speak

Mandarin at the US Foreign Service Institute in Arlington, Virginia, was almost a waste of time. You see, Mandarin is the official language spoken in Beijing. We were assigned to Guangzhou, one thousand miles to the south. In Guangzhou, the official language spoken is Cantonese. Yes, you guessed it. The State Department sent me to the wrong language class! If this mistake were made by a training division in the private sector, someone would probably lose their job. But in State, where mediocrity is the golden standard of performance, it didn't really matter.

Sometimes we went to the outdoor markets near our apartment building to look at all the *exotic proteins* offered for sale — snakes, turtles, frogs — all of which were kept in small containers, crawling all over each other. *Yeah, not very appealing!* There were exotic fish to buy and to eat, small alligators to consume, and plenty of crustaceans that looked like they were from another planet.

The real adventure was to try and make sense of a menu at a local restaurant. During the first few months, we were never sure what we were ordering until we were served. Very quickly did we learn restaurants do not readily serve cold water to patrons. Instead, the Chinese custom is to serve warm water to drink, not cold water. We soon realized the need to ask for *ice* in our water, but many times, ice was not served at all. It simply wasn't available unless the restaurant catered to Westerners. We eventually discovered that napkins are not offered to diners in restaurants. Instead of napkins, small packs of tissues were offered for sale, so we typically carried a pack of tissues with us when going out to dinner. We ate some of the best Chinese food while living in China, but also some of the worst!

Every day brought a new surprise as far as different customs and the mentality of the local people. Lack of personal space and blatant staring at us were high on the list of things that were making us uncomfortable, but we had to learn to live with it. Sometimes, we just had to laugh about the extremes, like standing in a line to pay for groceries. Locals acted as if we didn't exist, walking past us to get in front of us. We realized our mistake: we left space between us and the person in front of us, as is customary in western cultures, but not in China.

And let's not forget the crowds. You couldn't go anywhere without expecting it to be flooded with people. And everyone wore masks which covered their mouth and nose, believing it was protecting them from the terrible pollution hovering over the city, forming brown clouds just above our heads. To be honest, we found it comical, watching the locals with their face masks on. Little did we know that soon, the whole world would follow — except for different reasons.

* * *

By early November we were fully settled into our apartment, with our belongings from storage in Belgium having arrived by then. We were taking a trip to Hong Kong for my wife's birthday and were looking forward to the Marine Ball a week later. Daniela began learning to speak Cantonese by taking a weekly language class at the US Consulate while she waited for her security clearance to be finalized before she could start working in the HR section at the consulate.

Several months later, I received a call from an American colleague at the consulate. One of the American contractors, a janitor named Pete, didn't show up for work that day. It was Monday morning, and maybe the janitor overslept or was hung over from the weekend. Another janitor decided to go to his apartment to get him, but no one answered the door. Since all the apartments for American staff were rented by the American Consulate, the Facilities Manager requested an extra key to Pete's apartment from the front desk and went to Pete's apartment. Opening the door, he found Pete's lifeless body in bed. I found out when one of my agents called.

"Alex, they found Sneaky Pete. He was in his apartment."

"Well, that's good," I replied.

"Not really. He's dead."

Oh boy. I called to let the Consul General know what had happened and that DSS would open a death investigation. I followed that phone call with a call to Beijing to keep the RSO informed, and then I called DSS Headquarters in Washington, DC. Afterwards, I met up with the two DSS Investigators on my team in the lobby and we went to Sneaky Pete's apartment where we were joined by my locally hired Chinese Investigator, Ming, and the medical officer assigned to the consulate. I asked Ming to contact the police and have them meet us at Pete's apartment, all-the-while giving HQ updates on what the American doctor needed to do to prepare the body for turnover to the Chinese authorities, and steps I needed to take to conduct an initial death investigation. The Consulate's Management Officer got somewhat involved since this could turn out to be a diplomatic mess. Hell, if foul play was possible, then the FBI would be sent to post to lead the investigation, but as of now, it was a DSS matter, and we needed to ensure proper steps were taken before Pete's remains were returned to the United States and to his family for burial.

Following strict guidance from Washington, DC, my men and I spent the entire day conducting our investigation at Pete's apartment, attempting to discover how he had died. The medical officer and I took blood samples, a urine sample and ocular fluid samples from the body and packaged the specimens on ice in accordance with the proper standards designated by the medical field as well as the criminal investigation regulatory standards. The day turned into night, and we still had plenty of work to do.

The medical doctor and I wrapped Pete's body in a traditional Chinese fashion using lightweight cotton bound with gauze straps to ensure the body, or evidence, wasn't tampered with. The police arrived at the apartment but stayed in the hallway of the building until they had written authorization to enter the consulate-leased flat. It was two o'clock in the morning when I woke the Consul General and asked him to sign a diplomatic note granting my Chinese counterparts the authority to enter Pete's apartment and take the body to the morgue.

With formalities settled, the Chinese came in and carried him away, taking him to a local morgue where they insisted on conducting an autopsy to determine the cause of death. The State Department fought back, saying he was there under diplomatic privileges, and wanted to have the body transported to the US without the Chinese conducting the autopsy. Extensive diplomatic negotiations regarding how and when the body could be transported followed as the Chinese Government stood their ground. DSS was steadfast in this investigation, demanding the Chinese Government release the body. On the other hand, the Chinese Government made it clear they would not allow Pete onto any aircraft unless Chinese doctors conducted the autopsy in China. State caved.

I was asked to observe the autopsy, which I had done before in the US, so I knew how American doctors conducted the procedure, but I wasn't sure how Chinese doctors would go about it. In the end, the Chinese method was similar to US methods and acceptable under the circumstances. I informed DSS that, according to the professional opinion of a Chinese medical examiner, Pete had died from cardiac arrest. The Chinese Government was satisfied at last, and they handed him over to us.

The next day, Chinese officials loaded the body onto a China Southern aircraft, and I had one of my agents escort Pete's body back to Maine where a US autopsy was conducted. Several days later, we received word from the medical examiner in the US that the opinion of the American doctor's cause of death matched the Chinese doctor. Heart attack.

I had seen and done many things in my twenty-six-year career including arresting hundreds of people, protecting diplomats and princes, and witnessing autopsies. I had been a parole officer, conducted undercover operations, and broke my back during training, but I had never prepared a body for the morgue until that night.

* * *

Almost a year into my assignment, DSS scheduled a worldwide conference for all regional security officers to attend in DC. I thought this would be a good time for my family to travel back to the US with me and see friends, check on our house in Northern Virginia, and eat something besides Chinese food. A few days before the conference began, DSS canceled it, but as we already had flights purchased and everything was planned, we went anyway.

After spending ten days in the US, we checked our flight status out of Dulles International Airport and found that our airline bookings had been canceled. I wasn't sure why this happened, so I contacted the travel agency and was told that our seats were still booked on the original flight and there wasn't a problem. I then contacted United Airlines and spent hours on the phone, trying to figure out why we had tickets but not seats on the return flight back to China. After three nights of making phone calls to China Southern Airlines in Guangzhou from Washington in the middle of the night, United Airlines informed me the problem was resolved for the first leg of our flight — DC to New York — but as of now, our seats on the flight from New York to Guangzhou were *on hold*. Upon our arrival at JFK, we checked in with China Southern at the gate and were told to speak with the United Airlines customer service desk at JFK during our layover in New York.

United Airlines in JFK said the problem lies with China Southern Airlines and not United Airlines, and as of now, two hours before our flight back to China, we didn't have plane tickets. United told me to speak with the China Southern gate agent to see why we didn't have seats on the flight back to the far east, and I argued that I had already done that, and that China Southern had told me that we didn't have seats on the flight.

Before the gate opened and passengers began boarding the flight, the Chinese gate agent who worked for China Southern Airlines told me that they will straighten the problem out and get us on the plane, but it didn't happen. We showed our diplomatic passports, diplomatic visas, and Chinese Residency cards to the gate agent, informing her that we lived and worked in Guangzhou, but she still didn't allow us on the flight. Everyone had boarded the flight except me and my family, and the gate closed. The pilot had the plane door closed and was ready to taxi away from the terminal.

"Babe, the Chinese Government is hassling us again. If they don't let us on this flight, we're curtailing our assignment and not going back to China. We aren't going to keep dealing with these intrusions from the Chinese Intelligence Agency."

Then the phone rang. The gate agent picked it up and listened to the voice on the other end, then hung up the phone.

"Sir," she said in English. "You and your family can board now."

Relieved but still frustrated over our bad experience with China Southern Airlines, there was no doubt in my mind the Chinese Ministry of State Security, America's version of the CIA, had a hand in our temporary removal from the flight back to China. MSS was sending me a message; *We control you*. And they were right.

Once the gate door closes, I've never seen it re-opened to let a passenger on the aircraft until that day. Have you?

* * *

A few months later, I was scheduled to fly to Thailand for annual firearms training. Since the Chinese Government doesn't allow DSS Agent to qualify with weapons in China, I couldn't practice shooting my gun and had to travel to Bangkok once each year to shoot weapons with the Marines and *qualify*, meaning practice and shoot a passing score. Basically, it was a weekend trip paid for by the taxpayers, but it was also necessary to practice with various weapons on a regular basis so I could maintain my proficiency.

At the airport in Guangzhou, I checked a bag, presented my Diplomatic Passport to the Thai Airways representative at the counter, and headed for the security checkpoint. Putting my carry-on bag on the conveyor belt so that it could be x-rayed, I walked through the metal detector, and I grabbed my carry-on off the x-ray belt and began walking toward the gate.

"Sir! Wait a minute," a Chinese Police officer said to me in Cantonese. I turned to find out if there was a problem.

"Do you have any weapons in the bag?"

"No," I replied, surprised at the accusation.

"Can I have a look?"

"Yes, have a look."

The Chinese security officer looked through my carry-on which I packed with a book, noise-canceling headphones, an energy bar, change of clothes, and my iPhone. He pulled a bullet out of the bottom.

Oh shit.

"Sorry. I forgot that was there. You can keep it," giving him permission, as if he needed it, hoping this wouldn't turn into a larger issue.

"Sir, I need you to come with me."

"I'm an American Diplomat assigned to the US Embassy. As you know, I am the head of security in South China. I am on my way to Thailand and didn't realize I had the bullet in my bag. Am I free to go?"

"Sir, I need you to come with me."

"Officer, I need to get to the gate, my flight is departing soon."

"Sir, I need you to come with me," the police officer repeated a third time. "We will go to see my supervisor."

In case you're wondering how bad this situation was, anyone caught with a weapon or bullets in China can expect to spend years in prison. Six months earlier, an American traveling from China had packed a toy gun and plastic caps in his bag for his son back home in Kansas. The police detected the toy gun and caps, detained the man, and put him in jail. The guy was still in jail in China. So, to say that I was in serious trouble is an understatement. But I had diplomatic immunity, and I hoped this was enough to get me out of this jam.

The officer walked me to the airport police station and made a series of phone calls. I contacted my supervisor to let him know I had been detained, and this sparked somewhat of a shitstorm back in DC. The problem was, I was in the wrong. I brought it on myself and used my best negotiating skills to get out of the mess.

Speaking in Mandarin to the police at the station, I asked if I could go to the Thai Airways ticket counter and get on the next flight.

"No, you cannot leave," the officer insisted.

"Are you saying that I am not free to leave? That you are detaining me from taking my flight? Are you restricting me from going to the American Consulate?" I asked him, setting the stage for a potentially catastrophic and illegal detention by the Chinese Communist Party of an American Diplomat.

"Sir, you do realize that I am a diplomat and have diplomatic privileges," I continued. "You cannot detain me."

I sent a text to a Chinese contact I had at the Ministry of Foreign Affairs. She replied by text almost immediately.

"Alex, did you have a bullet in your carry-on?"

"Yes, I did. I didn't realize it was there. I'm on my way to Thailand for work and didn't know I had a bullet in my luggage. Can you have these guys let me go?"

"I'll see what I can do."

A few minutes later, the officer asked me to sign a document written in Mandarin. Since my reading skills were not quite reliable enough to read a legal document which could be an admission of guilt and land me in prison, I told the officer I can't sign anything. He assured me that he'd let me go if only I signed this document. I hesitated, thought about turning this issue up a notch by refusing to sign and walking out of the police station just to see what they'd do to me. I gave it a minute and considered two options. My first option was to sign the form and hope they'd let me go. If the document was an admission of guilt about carrying the bullet, I could be taken to prison tonight, and I'd probably spend the next several years in jail. It would likely become a major diplomatic incident which would include the US President getting involved. I wouldn't be able to see my wife and kids for God only knows how long, and my career would be over.

The other option was to not sign the document and hope they let me go. If I didn't sign it, would the police forgive and forget, or would they tackle me to the ground in the middle of the airport, take me to prison, convict me of espionage without a trial, lock me up in a horrible Chinese prison and throw away the key?

Considering both, I decided to risk it and I signed the form, even though I had no idea what it said. They did, indeed, let me go and I changed my flight to a later departure and made it to Bangkok later that night.

Wow, that was close.

* * *

Not long after I returned from Thailand for firearms training, we were ready to visit Vietnam, a vacation we had planned for months. When we arrived at the airport in Guangzhou, I mentioned to Daniela that I hoped this trip would go smooth and we weren't going to be hassled by the Chinese Police again. After all, the Chinese Intelligence Service had it in for me.

After we got out of the taxi and walked into the terminal where the China Southern ticket counters were located, I noticed a line of people with bags. Everyone was waiting to be screened for explosives before putting their baggage through a large x-ray machine. My family and I were pulled out of the line and around the x-ray machine, so I figured it was a courtesy they were providing to diplomats. We were directed to speak with a Chinese immigration officer.

"Sir, can I see your passports?" the officer asked in Cantonese.

"Sure, here you go."

The officer looked over the passports and motioned with her hand that we can proceed to the China Southern ticket counter to check-in for our flight to Phnom Penh. While walking toward the counter, another police officer asked where we were going, and I told her we were going to check-in with China Southern. I showed the officer our passports and boarding passes and she instructed us to stay there while she disappeared into a sea of travelers. *What now,* I thought to myself.

After a few minutes of waiting there by ourselves, in the middle of the busy terminal, we decided to walk twenty meters to our right and check-in with China Southern. As we were doing so, the officer showed up with three other Chinese Police officers, each of whom looked extremely agitated.

"Sir, why didn't you have your bags x-rayed?" the most senior officer asked. "Give me your passports," he demanded in Cantonese.

I did what I was told and gave the police officer our passports.

"I was waiting in line when your colleague called us out of line and checked our passports," I explained. "We don't mind having our bags searched. We are going on a holiday to Vietnam," I replied in

Mandarin. Since the two languages are somewhat similar, the officer understood me.

"You are visiting here?"

"No, we are not visiting. I am an American diplomat. I live here in Guangzhou. I am the head of security at the consulate," I said, handing him my Chinese residency card. "We were waiting in line and your colleague asked us to come around the checkpoint. She asked me to show her our passports. So, I did. She looked at them, gave them back to me, and said we could go. Now I'm here talking to you guys. What's the problem?"

The officer looked at our passports and diplomatic visas. He looked at my residency card, listing me as an American diplomat assigned to the consulate.

"What's the problem?" I repeated, tired of getting hassled every time we traveled into or out of China.

The officer handed our documents to me, turned, and stormed off, as if he was pissed that he didn't have a reason to detain an American traveler. But one officer remained behind. I turned to him.

"Can we go?" I asked.

He hesitated, then said, "You can go."

Frustrated for a few different reasons, I turned my back on the officer to check-in with China Southern, looking forward to getting away from the country for a couple of weeks while enjoying good food and the beautiful countryside in Vietnam.

* * *

It was December of 2019, and Daniela was pouring me a glass of wine one evening after work when she asked, "Did you see the telegram at work today about a virus in Wuhan?"

"Yeah, I did, but I wouldn't worry too much. There are all sorts of viruses and illnesses going around in this country," I casually stated, blowing off the notion that anything serious could come out of it. Of course, the Chinese Government had known about the virus for much longer than the rest of the 1.6 billion Chinese residents. Oh, and *Wikipedia* has it wrong — it was first discovered in October, not

December. Does a few months count? Sure, it does, but the US hadn't heard about the Wuhan outbreak in October. By January, though, the Chinese Government had all but quarantined the entire city of Wuhan, a city of twelve million residents — small by China standards. By then, the virus had surfaced in several countries, spread by humans traveling by plane from Wuhan to other parts of the world. That cat was out of the bag and couldn't be contained.

Travel restrictions to and from China were not put into place at that point, and we had an R&R trip planned for New Zealand and Australia later that same month. A few days after we landed in Christchurch, the New Zealand government restricted travelers entering their country from China, so we made it just in time to spend a holiday on the South Island.

My supervisor in Beijing called me one day while my family and I were having lunch overlooking Lake Wanaka, a deep lake with electric blue water hidden in the mountains.

"Alex, I realize you're on R&R now, but you need to know there is a talk about voluntary departure for the official American personnel and their families in the next week or so. If you don't make it back to China by the time it's announced, I'm not sure I can get it cleared by HQ to get you back to Guangzhou. So, you and your family probably aren't coming back to China anytime soon, unless you come back now."

A *voluntary departure* from a posting overseas refers to an option for American family members assigned to an embassy to be evacuated out of the country for several reasons. In this case, the voluntary departure was authorized because of the Wuhan virus. For those not in China at the time the voluntary departure was formalized, like me and my family who were in New Zealand, we were not permitted back to China. Instead, the State Department would fly us back to Washington, DC and pay our temporary living expense in corporate housing until it was safe to return to China and resume our assignment.

The timing of this virus outbreak couldn't have been any worse. It was late January 2020 when the most important of the Chinese holidays, the lunar new year, was celebrated on January 25, 2020. The

Chinese New Year festivities, which span over fourteen days, is a time for friends and family to get together, exchanging red envelopes filled with money. Red symbolizes luck and fortune in the Chinese culture, and that is why red envelopes, or *hóngbāo*, are used during the Chinese New Year. It is also one of the busiest times for travel. It's estimated that two billion people travel in and out of China and throughout Southeast Asia over a forty-day period to celebrate the lunar New Year. It is the largest migration of travelers in the world, and it was happening as the virus spread around the planet. But we didn't know at that time the virus would affect the entire planet.

Through this festive holiday, schools in China are closed and most of the country shuts down for several days to observe the Lunar New Year. It was summertime in the Southern Hemisphere, and the perfect time to travel to New Zealand and Australia, and it had been my wife's dream to visit since she was a child. We packed light, knowing it was summer and would be warm, but also trying to limit the amount of luggage we would have to worry about as we moved from one city to another.

After the initial phone call from Beijing, I relayed all the information to my wife, and we decided that we would not return to China before our vacation was over. We had this trip planned for a long time, and we didn't want to cut it short. Who knows when we would be able to come back? Can you blame us? No, we were going to see how the quarantine situation would pan out. *Whatever happens, happens.*

A few days later, we were in Australia when I received another phone call: "Alex, the embassy is making it official. As of tomorrow, family members and non-essential staff are being evacuated from China under *voluntary departure* status. For essential staff like yourself, and the others who are not in China right now, we need to get State Department approval to return to China. So, here's the deal; your wife and son can't return. Give me a couple of days and I'll find out if you're allowed to come back. If not, just go back to Washington and report to HQ. I'm not sure what type of work they'll have you do while you're there."

The last place I wanted to be was at headquarters until this pandemic ended. But then again, I'd be with my family, so there was an upside to it. A few days passed before I was told that the State Department (and probably the White House) approved of my return to China, and to work at the Consulate in Guangzhou. I was needed back, and I had to cut my trip short after all. *So much for a well-earned family vacation.*

My family, though, was not allowed to return to China, not even to gather winter clothes or other necessities they'd need in February. No medical records or school records. No winter coats and boots. Nothing. The State Department booked them on a flight to DC out of Sydney, Australia.

Preparing for this possibility during our vacation in Australia, we had already planned for my wife to pick up a rental car at the airport and arranged for a short-term apartment rental outside of DC. Since the house we owned in Virginia was being rented out, they couldn't stay there.

My wife drove me to the airport in Sydney and dropped me off before returning to the hotel for the next few days to enjoy the rest of the trip as much as possible, under the circumstances.

They never returned to China. Instead, they arrived at Dulles International on a cold and drizzly evening in early February 2020, without any winter clothing and only the items they had in their luggage. They started a new life in the US while I remained in China for the foreseeable future. We had no idea how long we would be apart, or what was to become of this.

After a long and tiring flight back to DC, with a layover in London where crowds were forced to stand in lengthy, twisting lines, undergoing extensive security measures, they arrived in the US and checked into their apartment near the train station in Tysons Corner, Virginia, an affluent neighborhood just outside of DC. Once again, Daniela had to come through on her own. Shopping for groceries, clothing, cosmetics, and other necessary items that were needed immediately was not an easy task when you are cold and jet-lagged, dragging around half-asleep kids. School enrollment turned out to be an even bigger deal than it should have been, as she didn't have any medical records, birth certificates, or immunization cards and other personal documents with her. Everything was in China. It took several weeks to get everything in order, and she managed to get my Mercedes Benz out of storage, which meant she no longer had to pay for the rental car. When everything was finally in place, she reported to work, taking the train to DC, resuming her duties in the HR office remotely.

The virus was spreading at an alarming speed, soon making its way to the US and other parts of the world. It seemed as though the world had changed overnight, and a mass frenzy had taken hold of people's lives in the US.

What had happened in China four months ago was now taking place in America. Schools were closed due to the virus, and school administrators had announced the students would be required to participate in distance-learning from home. With just one computer, my wife juggled home schooling with finding time to work remotely during the evenings and at night. Grocery shopping became an unpleasant task. She did her best to stock up on items when the shelves were nearly empty, limiting the store visits to once per week. Being confined to an apartment during the virus without any personal belongings or outdoor space — the apartment building was in the center of a business district — and nothing to keep her and the kids occupied was certainly not a fun experience for them. Their lives had been turned upside down, as it was for other families during the pandemic, but being on opposite sides of the world made it so much more challenging. She managed to take care of everything with me stuck in China, and it was five long months before we were reunited again.

Meanwhile, I was back in China where I encountered discrimination for being an American, a foreigner. The Chinese Government blamed the virus outbreak on the US military, American travelers, even travelers from the African continent. Dark-skinned people living in or traveling to China were condemned and not welcomed in restaurants. Many were even booted from hotel rooms and their own apartments!

All travelers arriving to China would be required to stay in a Chinese hospital for a two-week quarantine. Since the media in China is strictly controlled and monitored by the Chinese Government, the press reported only *government-approved* news and information to the Chinese citizens. The Chinese Communist Party spread propaganda that the virus didn't originate in China and instead spread *to* China from other countries. People believed it. Since online websites are severely restricted in China, citizens know only of what the government *allows* them to know. They are often-times fed fabrications of the truth, and this was taking place on a massive scale in China during the onset and spread of the virus, which later became known as Covid-19.

Residents and travelers throughout China were required to register with the Chinese Government, providing our names, addresses and phone numbers so we could be tracked anywhere in the country via phone signals. Yes, they certainly monitored our movements. As the days stretched to weeks and months, Americans were no longer welcomed at local and international restaurants due to this *foreign-borne disease.* The Chinese propaganda was in full swing.

Five months later, my assignment in China finally came to an end. It was time for me to say goodbye, forever, to a culture I had grown to love, and at the same time, despise. It was time to go home and hold my wife and squeeze my kids. The last few weeks prior to my departure were filled with uncertainty, however, as more and more flights out of China were canceled on a daily basis, and I found myself wondering if I would be able to leave as scheduled after all. Fortunately, I made it out of the country a few days before President Trump announced a travel ban on flights originating in China and arriving in the United States. I never returned to China.

For my next assignment, I was assigned to FBI Headquarters in Washington, DC, my top choice. And seven months later, I retired from the US Foreign Service with a pension, many great memories, and a headful of things I don't wish to remember. Although it was a great career and an honor to be an American Diplomat, I learned the US Government is not represented by the best and the brightest, not always. Make no mistake about it, most Foreign Service employees stumbled into their careers and traveled to places they would not normally be able to afford, made a very comfortable living, and will retire with a very, very nice pension. To be fair, though, there are some incredibly smart and hardworking people in this field, but in the overall ratio, unfortunately, they are a minority.

If you recall reading in the Preface, this book began more like my diary than my memoir. I wrote it so I wouldn't forget what happened in my past, but I also wrote it so I wouldn't need to remember. I got it out of my head and onto paper so I could sleep at night and let the past go. It was a fabulous career, experiencing people and places and events that you can only see on National Geographic or the Discovery Channel, or on the nightly news. For some agents, the job and the career define them as who they are in the world. I never wanted to be defined by my title or responsibilities or what I did for my country. I simply want to be defined as being a good father and husband. I'm still working on that, and I think this book has helped me get closer to that goal. Not being consumed with that lifestyle is new to me.

Ever since I can remember, my life, and the lives of my family, were always about what was coming next, instead of living in the moment. Not anymore. Time to tap the brakes.

13
My theory

After I retired, I wanted to do something different; something other than law enforcement, just to see if I could be successful at it. I got back into the public sector and health insurance. I studied for and passed my Series 6 exam to sell insurance packages to small businesses and was licensed in seven states. But I didn't have the drive and the joy in doing that type of work. *What do I really want to do. What would satisfy me, what am I good at?*

Every time I pondered this question, it always came back to my first true love: law enforcement. No, I decided not to get back into uniform and patrol the streets — I was too old to work nights and weekends again. Instead, I started my own security consulting business, *Viking Security Consulting LLC,* and work with the US Government and the private sector, offering my expertise accumulated over a twenty-six-year career in law enforcement and security.

I have lived in six countries, been to nearly eighty, and have finally answered my own question: *Was I fortunate to have known, at the age of five, what I wanted to do for the rest of my life?* The answer to me is as crystal clear as my wife's blue eyes and smiling face when she says she loves me. I was born to live the life I did. It wasn't easy; is life easy for anyone? But I did everything I ever wanted to do. No fear. No regrets. And for that, I feel fortunate. I always had something to prove. For years, I thought that meant proving to my family that I could succeed. It took me years to realize; I didn't need to prove anything to anyone except myself.

I recently spoke with a retired Marine who had spent some time helping fellow colleagues cope with Post-Traumatic Stress Disorder. He told me one of the things he asks his colleagues to do is put their thoughts on paper. I've always wanted to write a book, but this book is more than just about writing a story. It's about getting my thoughts out of my head. It's about coping with the stress that I've been through and dealing with the difficulties that I've faced, by seeing it on paper, living it, thinking about it, and realizing that I can let it all go. Let the stress out of my body, out of my head, free myself of all the burden so I can be *normal* again. So, I can feel exhilaration like I did when I was twenty or thirty. This book is for me, mainly. But at the same time, I wanted to share a few tales with you, and I hope you found some kind of enjoyment in reading it. I hope you laughed. That's what I'm trying to do more of these days. Maybe you learned a bit about the US Foreign Service and the dedication of the State Department. Perhaps you learned something new about yourself or gained a different perspective about life, and your experiences. Either way, thank you for reading my book.

As I look back at my career and my life, and all the things I had done and places I had been, and marrying my dream girl, I am reminded of something Patrick Swayze once said; he had done so much in life and experienced so many things, that he felt he had lived the lives of ten men. I think I'm like him in that regard. But not ten men. Try a hundred.

Slow roll.